Dangerous Toilets, Dollar Menus, Dirty Looks, and Discrimination

A Hard Look at Obesity in America

by Dr. William A. Dispoto

This book is dedicated to the memory of my mother Frances, who also suffered from this condition...

...to the rest of my family for their love and support...

...to all of my fellow obese Americans; this effort was made in your honor...never give up the fight!...

...and to the great people at BarIndustries, advocates for the obese and makers of the SK1000U wall mounted toilet support, for their kindness and courtesy in letting me use their photo as part of my cover art.

Table of Contents

Introduction: OK, it was MY fault, but I had help...!

OK, let's start by setting some ground rules. First, I am fat, and in varying degrees I have always been fat, and it's a pretty good bet that to some extent I might always BE fat. Even if I lose weight, since obesity is a disease like alcoholism, I will always be an obese person...I'll just be a "recovering" obese person. Second, I make no excuses for myself or how I got this way; I am not going to directly blame my glands, genetics, or McDonalds for my condition (although later I WILL explain how they all made it EASIER for me to get this way!!). I got this way because I AM A FOOD JUNKIE; I am a food addict...food is my drug of choice and I am hooked. I have had problems with other addictions in my life...I had a slight drinking problem when I was young, but I won that battle and am now proud to say that I never touch alcohol. I also smoked cigarettes for 15 years and was a two-pack-a-day smoker before successfully quitting in the 1990's. When it comes to the VICES in my life I am an abuser; it seems like I always use to excess rather than moderation. However, the ONE vice in my life that I have been unsuccessful battling is food...and that's because, unlike alcohol and cigarettes, I need it to live. As humans WE need food to live...it's our fuel. It's like oxygen, shelter, clothing, and human interaction...among the many things that are essential to our continued existence. Alcohol and tobacco are choices, but food is a basic human need. I can't just GIVE UP food like I did alcohol and cigarettes...I have to get my "fix" every day or sooner or later I will die. And like a drug addict, I want more of it every time I use.

That having been said, my obesity is my fault and is due to nothing more than my inability to find that fine line between "eating to live", which is good, and "living to eat", which is bad. No one held a gun to my head and forced me to overeat during those countless episodes of power eating and HUGE meals…I will only provide you with MY PERCEPTION of the TRUTH regarding obesity and fat-prejudice in society today: how I personally got this way, what it did to me and what it's doing to us, and why it won't go away unless we take action.

That having been said, being fat allows me some flexibility, some slack…and so does being the author of this book. In other words, don't expect me to sugar-coat this epidemic. I have LIVED it for 40+ years, so I'm going to say exactly what I WANT to say AND WHAT I THINK NEEDS TO BE SAID here. Maybe you too are overweight or obese…or maybe you are guilty of discrimination against the obese or of harboring ANY of the prejudices described herein…well, if that's true and you are easily offended, better gird your loins for a bumpy road…I am NOT apologizing for hurting your feelings, outing you as a fat-bigot, or telling the truth…!

In this book I will continuously use words like fat, obese, and overweight…and to a lesser degree words like rotund, chunky, heavy, gravitationally challenged (for the PC nuts), and just plain BIG. These words will be used interchangeably and in whatever context I am embroiled in at the time. Let's face it, you don't have to be fat to know the words used to describe us, so when you see one of them, you'll know what I'm talking about.

As I said, I'm fat but I am getting smaller. As of this writing, I am 49 yrs old (probably 50 or 51 by the time it's published) and I weigh somewhere just south of 500 pounds. That makes me "morbidly" obese in the eyes (and language) of the medical profession. That's the WORST category to be in, in case you didn't know it. There isn't a category of fat people that is worse than morbidly obese, or maybe the medical profession just hasn't thought up a name that is humiliating enough for people that are "larger than morbidly obese" yet. If being labeled "morbidly" obese isn't bad enough, maybe in the future the highest category will be called "monstrously" obese, or "suicidally" obese, or maybe "grotesquely" obese…how about "worldly" obese (pun intended), or maybe simply "a ticking time-bomb". Oh, there are plenty of embarrassing names that you can attach to obesity categories, but I'll leave that up to the medical "profession" (using that term loosely, hence the quotations); they are MUCH better at humiliation and degradation than I am.

Yes, I AM trying to be thinner…any fat person who tells you that they are HAPPY and CONTENT with their current condition is either lying or has given up; sorry if that means YOU…! Sure, I have read a lot of the fat-acceptance literature (i.e., "accept yourself the way you are and just be happy…!") and I have read a LOT of the literature released by the leaders of organizations that fight prejudice against fat people (more on that in later chapters) and support the advancement of the obese-agenda, but that doesn't mean I agree with everything they propose. I DO like myself, but I AM NOT happy and I am NOT CONTENT with the way I am…there's a BIG difference between liking yourself and being happy with yourself. I am NOT as happy as I can be, and supreme happiness is my ultimate goal. That is why I am constantly battling my weight, because I know that my weight, while not affecting my ability to function as a human being in society, is adversely affecting my health and is keeping me from doing a lot of things that I enjoy doing. However, my struggle with me weight does NOT diminish the reason for why I felt this book needed to be written…or why I felt what is about to be said NEEDED to be said…so that's why I put pen to paper (or better stated, fingers to lap top) to write this book.

Most of you who read this book will probably find some humor in it, but that's OK because I specifically wrote it in that tone; the finished product is more enjoyable and readable I think. But let me stress that I am only making fun of my own situation, my own life experiences; if you find some humor in it, then I have accomplished what I set forth to do. I EXPECT you to laugh, especially those who share my affliction for I hope they may take from my experience some solace with their own struggles. In other words, I am not making fun of fat people and what they have to endure on a daily basis: I am simply holding a mirror up to my life and letting you look at me, and then yourself. If you find humor in what I write, ask yourself why you think it's funny. Hopefully, by the time you reach the end of this book that urge to laugh will change to a feeling of respect, understanding, acceptance, and toleration.

Chapter 1: A personal history of being fat - The Early Years

My problems date all the way back to the day I was born, January 18, 1961. My dad loves to tell the story of my birth and how I held (and did for years) the record as the biggest male baby born in that hospital in Northern New Jersey. I was almost 11 pounds when I was born, and even though I was my mom's second baby I think I gave new meaning to the term "labor pains". My dad recalls the looks and stares I got as I lay there in the nursery...how the new dads were ignoring their own kids as they stared at the freakishly huge kid in the basinet with my family's name. My father remembers that most of those other dads thought I was several months old because I was almost twice the size as the other babies. Like so many obese people, I am <u>genetically</u> <u>predisposed</u> to be obese...it's in my DNA fingerprint...making it harder for me than a normal person to maintain a healthy weight. I was cursed from birth, and according to my parents already living in the obese "fishbowl" that has become our society.

My memories of growing up are, like most people's, scarce but vivid. I was a chronic bed-wetter until late in my childhood...is there any connection there? I took longer to potty train than most...not sure if that means anything...and I sucked my thumb for years until one of my brothers "outed" me to one of my friends (a HUGE controversy and cause of friction between us at the time!!)...I was smart, conceited, elitist, and stubborn as I grew up and I had one helluva temper...basically your run-o-the-mill, know-it-all Irish/Italian demon child.

For the first 12 or 13 years of my life I was a "chubby" kid, I LOVED to eat, and I was the LEAST picky eater of my siblings. The exact opposite of my brothers and sister…while they would drive my mom nuts with their food likes and dislikes, there was almost NOTHING I would not eat. OK, admittedly I couldn't handle canned peas and lima beans (still hate them…sorry pea and LB farmers!)…I hated fish (for a while, but love it now)…have never touched liver in ANY form…and never acquired a taste for lamb, but everything else was fair game…! I would always ask for second helpings no matter what the dish, and sometimes thirds too. My mom and dad made sure that we were served healthy, nutritious food…the ONLY mistake they made, with me especially, was that they sometimes wouldn't tell me NO when I asked for more…if there was food on the table and no one else wanted it, I could have it, eating basically until I was full.

I remember eating like that all of the time. My dad would leave us lunch money every day, just enough for the school-priced lunch…and I would constantly ask for more because I was buying extra food in the lunch line...in the form of snack cakes, ice cream, and candy. When I was in elementary school during intramural basketball season I would buy donuts from the local bakery around the corner from the gym…I was the world's WORST B-ball player, and I think I just joined the league for the donuts…then in middle high school I would buy burgers from the local Burger King during band practice and when a McDonalds AND a Wendy's opened down the street from our house…yes, a McDonalds AND a Wendy's RIGHT DOWN THE STREET FROM US…not even a 5 minute bike ride…I would supplement my meals with endless burgers, milk shakes, and every other item on the menu. You know, sometimes I think God painted an "obese" target on my back from birth just for fun!

Then when I got to high school, during the winter season when I was not involved in an activity I would come home and watch soap operas while enjoying several huge peanut butter and jelly sandwiches, maybe some chips, maybe some snack cakes, and a big glass of whole milk only a few short hours before dinner. In my last 2 years of high school I played varsity football and our team would get together on Friday nights to watch game films of the team we were playing the next day…and during those sessions the coach would have fresh made pizzas brought in while we watched…and I would make sure to have a whole pizza all to myself…and this was only a few short hours AFTER I ate dinner at home…! In my defense the Friday night pizzas were NOT my fault; the coach required our attendance and one of the guys had a relative in the pizza business, and for 5 dollars we could get a whole pizza each…man I LOVED Friday nights…even more than game day!

My eating disorder didn't stop there…it became so much a part of my life and my behavior that I didn't think about it much…and either my friends didn't notice it or they just felt embarrassed to comment. From the ages of 10 through 17 I alternated from chubby to average and back to chubby…at my heaviest (sophomore year) I weighed about 220 lbs., but I usually alternated from the mid 180's to around 210 during football season. I DO have a big frame…short legs, long torso, slightly above average in height…so I carried the weight well as long as I stayed active. In my last 2 years of high school I played 2 sports per year with winter being my only off-season but I lifted weights for spring track season so I stayed pretty active year long. Once I got into my junior year I filled out my frame and looked OK.

I just remember eating all of the time…it became part of daily routine. I usually skipped breakfast…to this day I am still not a breakfast eater; my digestive system just does not wake up until sometime after 10 am…I know this is bad, but I have a hard time forcing myself to eat, especially when I am so willing to eat the rest of the day. But back in those days…once lunchtime hit…any chance I got to eat I would take it. Those were the days when the drinking age in NJ was 18, so I was doing a lot of drinking too. Drinking became to me what I understand marijuana is to those who enjoy it: it gave me the munchies! Alcohol actually made me hungry. So whenever I drank, I would eat…chips, jerky, burgers, pizza, candy and cake…anything I could get my hands on I would eat.

And since my system was able to handle it, I wouldn't think anything of chowing down on candy bars by the handful…four or five at a time…whole pizzas…several foot-long hoagies at a sitting…dollar burgers from McDonalds by the sackful. I remember going on band competitions and my mom and dad allowing me to go to the local Italian deli to buy a lunch…those lunches would consist of 2 foot-long Italian subs, a 10 oz. bag of chips, sometimes a pound of potato or macaroni salad, maybe cole slaw, several packs of Tastykakes (Krimpets and peanut butter KandyKakes were my favorites), and a 2 liter of something, usually Coke. Looking into my lunch bag you would think I was packing for a week-long canoe trip down the Rio Grande, but most of these competitions would only last 5 or 6 hours including travel. And when I got home…you guessed it…dinner, or a snack, or something that my mom kept warmed up for me…or leftovers from the fridge.

Up to this point you might be thinking "Why didn't your mom and dad do anything about your eating?" To tell the truth, as I entered my teens they did show concern but I was never really FAT during those earlier years, just chubby…and when I did get heavy they would certainly make their opinions known, especially my dad. My mom, God Rest her soul, had a weight problem too, and I grew up in an Italian-Irish house…the focus was on the kitchen, the family eating together, and eating was a good thing. Those were the days before we really knew what having bad eating habits would mean to us in our future lives. That was my problem; it was during that period in my life when I developed many of the bad eating habits that I exhibit today, and like the old saying goes my age finally caught up with me…gradually at first, then it fell on me like the proverbial ton of bricks.

When I left home for college I could have seen trouble right away if it hadn't been for the fact that I went to a school that had height and weight guidelines. I attended the US Military Academy at West Point NY, and for those of you who don't know, our military has strict guidelines for the physical conditioning of its service members. In fact, when I applied to the academies (I applied and was accepted at the Coast Guard Academy, the Merchant Marine Academy, and West Point, but West Point was my first choice) I was required to lose about 15 or 20 pounds during my senior year in order to pre-qualify for enrollment. My father, who was the school's superintendent (aka, "the boss") got me special permission to leave school grounds and go home where my mom prepared special meals for me from a diet developed by our school nurse, herself a former Army nurse! Talk about serious dieting! Anyway, after several weeks of lunches consisting of "3 ounces of cheese" or "4 ounces of dry tuna" I achieved my goal weight, was subsequently weighed and certified by the school nurse (I started to feel like a prize fighter by this time)…the nurse even had to go as far as to sign a notarized document confirming my success, which was sent to the Academy's Department of Physical Education. Luckily all of this occurred long before spring track season, since I needed to bulk back up for my role as one of the school's weight men (shot-put and discus)…but don't tell the academies!

So I get to West Point thinking that all of my troubles are over, but to my disappointed surprise I found that maintaining my weight at West Point was harder than it was at home. I remember a miscellaneous UNCONFIRMED statistic from my academy days that went something like this: it was estimated that the average male cadet ingested about 4000 to 6000 calories a day, significantly more the average of 2900 calories that most experts say is needed to maintain an acceptable weight. No wonder I had a hard time maintaining an "ideal" weight; I had 6000 calories a day shoved under my nose, and as anyone dieting knows, it is much harder to diet when the food is "in your face".

The food in the Academy Mess Hall was served family style and each course, from main to starchy sides to veggies, came in sufficient quantities that most of the people sitting at the table (there were typically 10 cadets per table) could have seconds and sometimes third helpings of everything! Even if you were "watching what you ate", a small serving was about the same amount of food that you might expect to find in 2 commercially-prepared frozen diet meals like Weight Watchers or Lean Cuisine. When I first got to the Academy as a freshman I was required to attend every meal (upper classmen do not have to attend breakfast) and I made sure I ate well at each sitting. To make things worse, in my first semester of my first year I joined the men's indoor and outdoor track team and things really went south…! I was on the weight team, just like high school, except this time I was throwing the shot put (indoor and outdoor), the hammer (outdoor) and the 35-lb indoor weight (the indoor version of the hammer throw). Since we were in training and were expected to bulk up and maintain our strength during both seasons, the varsity sports tables traditionally served double portions to certain members of each team, and I was one of those certain members. During my time on the varsity track squad (in deference to my fellow alum, we called them corps squad) I was being fed up to 10,000 calories a day!!! That's more than 3 times as many calories as the normal man is supposed to ingest per day to maintain a healthy weight.

So how did I make it through that year and a half (I was cut from corps squad in the middle of my second year because of a recurring back injury) without gaining 300 lbs? Well, the first thing the unfamiliar reader must know about the academy is that the academic buildings are quite a distance apart, and it is not unreasonable that a cadet might have a very brisk 10-minute walk between classes. There were 4 class hours in the morning and 4 again in the afternoon, so if you had 4 classes per day, 2 during each half of the day, and including walks from your room and back for lunch and again for dinner, a cadet could cover somewhere in the vicinity of several miles during the day. Then if you factor in mandatory intramural athletics (for those NOT on varsity sports or clubs), mandatory marches and parades, and just walking around socially, you can see how easy it is for a cadet to burn off the near 6000 calories he/she might get at a normal table. Varsity athletes are of course in training; I lifted weights every day for several hours during training and did several more hours of practice throwing and form drills. That resulted in the short term ability to burn off massive quantities of calories during that period in my life…I just wish I could do the same now.

So you must be saying to yourself by now "So that HAD to be it, right Bill?" Not even close…! It seemed like I was NEVER satisfied with how much food I was getting, even on the varsity sports tables with their double portions. I can remember conducting "food raids" after each meal; a food raid was a pet name I had for the practice of walking through the mess hall after a meal and collecting up all of the untouched and edible leftovers at the empty tables…! Even on the days when the mess hall served something very popular for the meal, like egg sandwiches and large coffee cakes for breakfast, burgers or pizza for lunch, and steak for dinner, there was ALWAYS something leftover on the tables if you looked hard enough. What made it a raid was the fact that there were dozens of other hungry food scavengers looking for leftovers too, and the successful raiders were the ones who got to the leftovers first. Now another little known fact about West point, at least back in the early 80s when I attended, was that no one was allowed a refrigerator in their room, even the upperclassmen. Food brought back from the mess hall had to be:

1. Easy to carry…for example, I loved the mess hall's version of Shepherd's Pie, but it didn't travel well wrapped in a napkin…oh yes, I forgot to mention…we weren't allowed to keep storage containers like Tupperware in our rooms either!

2. Small enough and easy to store on a window ledge…no fridges, in the room or anywhere else, and no cooked food allowed in the room during inspection hours, which were basically 24/7, and

3. During the warm days of late summer/early autumn and spring it had to keep well in warm temperatures

So there I was…eating enough food for three average college students, burning off as many calories as the same number of average college students, and I was looking for extra food at every meal during my first 2 years. I especially remember the pies and cakes they would serve…the Academy has its own full-service bakery in the mess hall, and fresh baked goods were produced for about 4000 cadets 3 times a day…the cakes and pies were baked and served in the same piece of cookware…big 12 inch steel pie pans which yielded 10 above average sized slices but more typically 8 HUGE slices of pie or cake. I say that because a lot of the cadets had learned, way before I did, that you got enough calories from just eating a normal single serving at each meal WITHOUT dessert…so many of the upperclassmen skipped desserts, leaving more for the people at the table during the meal, and if it wasn't scooped up then, leaving more for the food raiders after the meal. "Borrowing" the metal pans back to your room was, to the best of my memory, frowned upon but NOT against the rules as long as you returned them in a reasonable amount of time…so I can remember many a food raid when I would scavenge 2, 3, or more full 12 inch pans of coffee cakes, custard pies, fruit pies, mousse pies, etc…yes, WHOLE PIES…and I would bring them back to my room for storage until the late evening hours…which included the time from after dinner to morning formation during which I had little or no access to food. Sometimes I would do this at breakfast AND lunch if there was room on my window ledge. I don't even want to think about how many calories I ingested from those days…it makes me dizzy and sick at the same time…!

So back to our math lesson…if I was eating just as much as I was burning WITHOUT the extra food I would bring back to my room…and keep in mind that pies and cakes were only 2 of the many edible targets of my scavenging missions…I also loved main courses too, if I could find them…what do you suppose happened to me after eating the extra food? If you do the math right…yup, more going in than coming out…so to speak…so I began to gain weight. My custom fitted uniforms began to get tight and then didn't fit me, so I had to get some larger uniforms made for me. It was all overlooked at first because I was a varsity athlete…and at West Point just like at so many of your bigger schools…varsity athletes were almost untouchable. As long as I attended class and got passing grades, followed the rules and didn't get into too much trouble, I was allowed to get as big as I wanted to during the seasons…and unlike football players whose season ends usually around New Year's, the varsity track team practiced all year long…in the fall we practiced for the winter indoor season…no sooner did the indoor season end then we started practicing for the outdoor spring season…and the cycle just repeated itself.

So NOW you must be thinking that I have exhausted all of the opportunities to eat while at West Point, but you would be wrong. As if the mess hall didn't give me enough chances to ruin myself there were other places where a hungry cadet could get his/her food fix. The first place which brings back mixed memories of good times and horrible behavior was the on-post pizzeria known as Mama Brava's. Again, for those of you who are unfamiliar with the academy it should be noted here that the cadets are treated like, for lack of a better comparison, prisoners in a jail. They are restricted where they can go and when. During the day we were restricted to the school grounds; almost everywhere is within limits as long as you are on base. At night during study hours you are severely limited where you could be; you HAD to be in academically conducive place; they included your room or the room of a friend if you were studying together, the library, the computer lab (this was before laptops and PCs in every room), or for the upperclassmen the company day room watching TV. Since we were not allowed off post in the evenings, the only places where a guy could get something to eat once the mess hall closed were the places on base, and Mama Brava's was the base' only authorized pizzeria. They made subs, pizzas, Italian dishes, and calzones, and during the night you were allowed to walk over to MB's as long as you were back before taps (aka, lights out).

You might be asking yourself "Why would anyone want to spend money on pizza when they had access to such a great source of free and excellent food like the academy mess hall?" I don't know what motivated most cadets, but my reason for frequenting MB's as often as I did was born out of pure laziness. One of the rules about eating in the mess hall was that you were required to dress in uniform when you ate there, and on the weekends that meant one of the many formal uniforms we had, not the comfortable shirt and slacks we would dress in during the week when we attended class. So since I was too lazy to get showered and dressed in my dress grays or whites on the weekends, I would just buy a quick meal from MB's, where I could wear something as simple and comfortable as my gym clothes to pick my food up…!!

Oh, and the meals I would buy from MB's were the stuff of legends…!!! On the weekends when I had nowhere to go and I was stuck on base, I would buy these huge meals…to this day my friends can't believe how much food I would eat in one sitting during one of those sessions. My typical Saturday meal from MB's consisted of one or two 12" subs, usually Italian or meatball parmesan; a large pizza, usually with pepperoni, onion, and extra cheese; a pepperoni calzone; an Italian dinner, my favorite was their lasagna; and to wash it all down, a six-pack of diet Mountain Dew (of course diet…you didn't expect me to make a PIG of myself did you? Besides, I was watching my weight and didn't want to overdo it…!). These eating sessions became known as "power eating" sessions, a phrase coined by my roommate Billy Groeger, one of my best friends in the world who died tragically in a car accident back in 1986. Billy called them power eating sessions because of the strained look that would come over my face when I was eating; Billy would say it looked like I was expending a lot of effort just to eat, kind of like the look a power lifter gets when he is concentrating on a heavy lift. The name stuck, and to this day whenever I binge I call it a power eating session. There were usually some leftovers from my MB sessions, but not enough to make another full meal…but luckily for me I was so full after one of these sessions that I would not get the urge to eat again until Monday. If I ate anything on Sunday it was something light from breakfast in the mess hall…a quick shower and slap on the dress grays and pop into the mess to steal a coffee cake or a few bacon-egg-cheese sandwiches to sneak back to my room before anyone realized that I hadn't shaved or combed my hair…and I was set for the day.

So that covers our meals and our junk food, but what about munchies? Where could a hungry raider get his fix of candy, snack cakes, or ice cream? Well West Point had that figured out too, in the form of a place called the Boodler's; it was a small cadet-only candy/snack store located on base among the barracks (aka, living quarters). There is a long history behind the Boodler's, and there isn't enough room here to discuss it; suffice to say, it was a long standing tradition that a cadet with a sweet tooth could get what they needed at the Boodler's. For me, it was like a home away from home; I patronized the B's at least 3 or 4 times a week during the year…I especially liked the fact that it was one of the few places on base where a guy could get a pint of ice cream, and the B's went through a LOT of ice cream every week…! Since they didn't have my favorite flavor (Baskin-Robbins Pralines and Cream…!), I would typically choose Rocky Road…the only problem was that ice cream had to be eaten immediately and all in one sitting…no fridges, remember? But you could also get candy, snack cakes (except back then the Philadelphia-based TastyKake Company had not reached as far north as West Point New York, so I was left without my Butterscotch Krimpets, Peanut Butter KandyKakes, and Coconut Juniors…!), chips of all kinds, and other assorted goodies.

Combining the caloric horsepower of the mess hall, Mama Brava's, and the Boodler's and what you got was a formula for dieting catastrophe. My weight varied from the mid-180s to as much as the low 200s, which may not sound like a lot unless you consider that my maximum allowable weight, according to the height-weight charts that the academy used, was around 187 pounds…my IDEAL weight was more like 165 to 167 pounds…! Hell, I weighed more than that when I was in the seventh grade…!! I was constantly flirting with the max weight for my height…so if I couldn't fix my weight, what I needed to do was fix my height…!! I was about 5 feet and 9 and a half inches tall, but during the weigh in's the person taking the measurements would round down to the nearest whole inch…my max weight for 5'9" was 187 pounds, but for 5'10" it was a much more reasonable (and attainable) 192 pounds. I tried everything I could to ensure I measured "five-ten"…when I knew a measurement was being conducted I would lay in bed for as long as I could before the weigh in (because someone told me that your backbone stretched when you laid down) and just before I went downstairs to get measured I would hang from a pull up bar in a friend's room to try and get that extra quarter-inch of stretch…and it usually worked, except when they sprung surprise weigh-in's on us and I had no time to prep…then I was screwed…!!

By my junior year I knew I needed to do something because my varsity career was over due to injury and there was a nasty rumor going around that if any cadet failed their height-weight measurements three times in any single year they would be subject to dismissal…I averaged 2 failures a year, usually when the measurements were taken after holidays when I would come back from several weeks of my mom's cooking..!! I barely made it out of the second semester of my sophomore year (I failed twice and was dangerously close to failing a 3rd time in the same semester), so at the beginning of my junior year, after yet ANOTHER height-weight failure and an ominous warning from my company Tactical Officer (a regular Army officer who was in administrative charge of a company of about 120 to 150 cadets), I decided to do something. I went on a radical diet during the first semester of that year which consisted of eating only twice a day…lunch and dinner…and the only thing I would eat was the main course. No carbs, no desserts, and usually no veggies. No trips to the pizzeria or the snack bar either; this was never confirmed but I heard that Mama Brava's sent out scouts to see what happened to me, and the Boodler's sent out an APB because they thought I was kidnapped…! I starved, but it worked: by the time I went home for Christmas vacation in December I weighed about 167 pounds. When my mom and girlfriend saw me they cried…literally CRIED…as I said earlier, I have a big frame and 167 pounds was just too thin for me, so I looked like I had just walked out of a concentration camp…! I also hated the way I looked, but I do have some fond memories of that short period in my life: I could finally wear the type of stylish clothes that I was always just a few pounds too heavy to wear. That was back in the skin tight "designer jeans" 80s, so I bought myself a pair of 32" waist Calvin Klein's (at least I think they were CKs), had the inseam custom-tailored for me, and I wore those pants until they almost disintegrated and returned to dust by themselves…!

Despite my short term success, I battled with weight issues for the next 2 years…during the school semesters I was able to maintain an acceptable weight by dieting and massive amounts of exercise, but as soon as I went home for holidays or weekends and was exposed to my mom's cooking I would gain weight and would spend weeks trying to lose it, hoping that there would not be a weigh-in while I was trying to lose. It became an ongoing battle with the department of physical education, the folks who were in charge of the weigh in's and conducted the physical conditioning tests during the year. A little known program to folks who are unfamiliar with the academies is the rigid physical fitness program for the students. We had to take phys ed classes every semester during the year, we were also required to participate in intramural athletics during the year (not including varsity sports athletes), and finally we had to take 3 physical fitness (PT) tests each year. In the fall was the 2-mile run test (conducted in Army boots my 1st two years then switched to running shoes after that), in the winter was the indoor obstacle course test, and in the spring was the Army Physical Readiness Test (fondly referred to as the APRT). I could waste a lot of space here describing these tests, but for the out of shape (like me) I'm afraid even WRITING about them might cause me to have a coronary incident…! During your years at the academy your phys ed grade is based on a combination of the grades you receive in your phys ed classes AND your performance on the PT tests. More emphasis is put on the PE class grades during your early years but the emphasis swings from PE class grades to the three PT tests during your later years…until your senior year when your WHOLE physical fitness grade is based on those three damn PT tests…!! I STRUGGLED with each test every year, earning just enough credit to BARELY pass phys ed each year…in fact, I don't think I earned a grade in phys ed higher than a "C" in any semester during my four years. Basically it was a four-year chase…me running and the department of PE chasing me…and by the grace of God they never caught me, but I heard footsteps for four long years…!!

Sooner or later everyone has that recurring dream (nightmare?) about being back in school…some people envision themselves naked in front of their fellow students, some folks find themselves back in a class that they struggled with, maybe taking an exam after having forgotten everything about the subject. My nightmare is similar but WAY more intense and vivid…and I have been having this nightmare every so often for the past 25 years…I am back at the academy after a summer vacation but I am NOT the cut-out tin soldier size I was back then…I am the size I am now, all 500 pounds of me. I arrive in civilian clothes and I try to fit into my uniforms and nothing will fit…even my gym clothes won't fit. Usually in the dream I am able to run and exercise and sometimes I am able to lose the weight before classes start, and during those episodes I awake feeling refreshed and calm…but sometimes I am unable to do anything about the weight…the first day of classes approaches and I begin to panic. I live the nightmare right up to walking into class in my underwear before I wake up feeling panicky, nervous, miserable, and anxious.

I didn't fare much better when I finally graduated and entered the US Army. Granted, I was finally free of one set of difficulties…the opulence of the West Point mess hall, the convenience of Mama Brava's and the Boodler's…but out on my own I was presented with a whole NEW set of issues…call them temptations or obstacles if you will. For example, while food was no longer free like it was in the WP mess hall, I was now earning a salary…it admittedly wasn't a very BIG salary by 1980's standards, but it was sufficient for my lifestyle. I also got what the Army called "quarters" and "subsistence" allowances…fancy terms for extra money to pay for food and a place to live. A smart young lieutenant could always find a clean, moderately priced one-bedroom apartment at most Army bases and, with the possible exception of utility bills (phone, cable, and electric), the "quarters" allowance could cover the cost. So basically, as far as a "roof over my head" was concerned, I was essentially living for free.

The food allowance was a different story; what the Army paid an officer each month for food was equal to what the officer would pay for three meals a day in a mess hall (yes, after we became officers, food was no longer free in the mess halls…we had to pay for it). This is not a bad deal, but no young lieutenant wants to spend his time eating in a mess hall three times a day, ESPECIALLY on the weekends. He/she is now on their own…free from family and college…independent…so they want to eat on the local economy…! Fast food places, maybe a nice sit down restaurant meal every now and then…and definitely cooking for themselves whenever possible. Unfortunately the allowance didn't allow for retail prices in most cases…if I remember correctly I got somewhere around $130 a month as a second lieutenant, which was a little more than $4 a day, so it certainly wasn't enough to eat fast food 3 times a day, even once a day. BUT DID WE CARE??!! Of COURSE not…we were enjoying our freedom and even if we had to spend a small portion of our salary for food…wasn't that what our civilian peers were doing…those unlucky men and women who graduated from civilian schools and got real jobs in the real world? They were making a LOT more money than we were, but they were paying for high priced apartments, furniture, food, and maybe even parking…so we knew we had it pretty good.

My bad eating habits followed me into the Army…and the only thing that kept me honest (and kept me from ballooning up during my early to mid 20's) was the army's physical fitness program, the fitness tests we had to pass each year (yup…I escaped the West Point Department of Physical Education but I didn't escape the fitness requirements), and…GULP!!...Army height-weight standards. The army had them too, but as I remember it they were not nearly as strict as the standards at West Point. What it boiled down to was this: most army units had a structured PT program in which everyone was expected to participate TOGETHER…but some units allowed officers to conduct their own PT program independently…and only occasionally participate in unit runs. Those were the units I liked…the ones that let me do my own thing…which often amounted to NOTHING…but what I NEEDED was a unit that held my feet to the fire and forced me to stay in shape. Also, once a year we had to pass the Army Physical Readiness Test (The same APRT that we had to pass at West Point every spring) and several times a year we had to get weighed in, but the weigh ins were loosely coordinated and often not monitored, so a clever lieutenant could sometimes indefinitely postpone and sometimes even avoid completely a scheduled weigh in. What he/she could NOT avoid was that dreaded APRT, because the results were posted in your army file and were used as part of the army promotion program. If you wanted to get promoted, you had to take the test…and as you climbed the ranks of the army, if you wanted to get promoted to the HIGHER ranks, not only did you have to take the test but you had to do WELL in the test! It was a relatively simple test: as many pushups and sit ups as you could do in 2 minutes for each exercise and a 2 mile run in sneakers as fast as you could make it. Running was never my strong suit (with a leg inseam around 28 inches, could you blame me? I had legs like fire hydrants…!) and sit ups were my Achilles heel…hell, even though I was pretty good at pushups I wasn't good enough to offset my limitations in the other 2 events. So…during my four years in the army I struggled much like I did at the academy…trying to maintain my weight for the weigh ins I couldn't avoid, trying to stay in shape enough to at least pass the annual APRT's…and hoping that I would be assigned to a unit that let me develop my own exercise regimen…and I was pretty lucky in that respect. I took a lot of temporary duty assignments…one close to Death Valley CA for six months, one in Honduras Central America for six months to name a few…because those assignments often had specific missions and long work hours, which left little time to structure or maintain a formal PT program…which means I was left alone. Other assignments, like my year in South Korea, were less desirable. Whenever I was assigned to a company commander who was on one of those physical fitness kicks I would go through hell…usually resulting in extra PT during my off-duty hours to get in the shape HE wanted me in. I remember specifically my company commander in Korea and then my 1st company commander when I returned from Korea and was assigned to Foot Hood

Texas…both of them were jocks (I HATED working for jocks…!) and were not satisfied with any of their officers just being "average"; they wanted us to be marathon runners…! During those years it seemed like all I ever did was run…morning, then again in the afternoon, weekends…it got so bad that I would always have a clean set of gym clothes with me 24 hours a day just in case I needed to go through a quick change for an unscheduled run…! But I made it…in 1987 I was honorably discharged from the army and came back home…and that was when my troubles REALLY started…!

Chapter 2: History continued: from the Army to the present and dangerous toilets!

Funnily enough, my first full-time job out of the army was a job with the US Air Force at an east coast airport as their Air Force liaison. It was a job that a friend recommended I apply for, and the guy in charge was a fellow West Point grad himself…which made it easy to get my foot in the door. I interviewed for the job relatively soon after I separated from the army, so I was in pretty good shape: five ten, about 190 pounds, and physically fit. I got the job but I also found out that my start date had to be delayed…that was when my troubles started.

To occupy my time and make some pocket money until my AF job started, I took a part-time job as assistant stock room clerk at a local hospital…BIG mistake. I was a cocky kid, all of 26 years old and full of PERCEIVED self-confidence…I took the job but felt it was beneath me. I mastered the intricacies of the job in about 2 days (truck comes in, unload, stock shelves, collect paper order sheets, fill carts, and deliver supplies to hospital departments…LATHER-RINSE-REPEAT) and immediately began to question authority. Keep in mind that this was the first chance I had in more than 25 years to question anybody…up to this point in my life it was following the rules of one person or another: my parents, my teachers, the West Point upperclassmen, and the officers appointed over me. When I took the hospital job I was finally FREE, or at least I thought I was…and I had 25 years of challenging "the man" saved up in my head. I took every opportunity to make trouble for people…sure, I thought I knew it all (as does everyone at that age) and no one could tell me what, who, where, or why.

There was one man in particular who disliked me and my brash manner…as I remember it, he was the head of engineering for the hospital but was also on the board of directors…making him "the boss". He was an older man, in his late 50s maybe early 60s, and he didn't like ANYONE who didn't bow to him when he walked by. To me he was nobody, even after my boss who was in charge of supply warned me that the guy was NOT one to be messed with. Of course I didn't listen, so I looked for every opportunity to confront this guy…I remember he liked to be called "sir", so every chance I got I just said hello or hi to him like I had known him for years, and each time he got angrier and angrier. Since formal greetings were not part of the hospital protocol there wasn't much he could do to me, but I certainly stayed in his mind.

Then one day, not long before my air force job started, something funny-and-tragic happened which is why I am writing about it here…and it sets up a pattern for many of the problems I have had since. He came down to the stockroom and he was up in arms about something…something that was supposed to be delivered somewhere and had not been, and he wanted someone to JUMP and get it done immediately. I was pushing an empty cart from a morning delivery, and he confronted me in the hallway where we left the empty carts. He started to yell at me as if what he wanted done was my fault, and politely and calmly I tried to explain to him that I had no idea what he was talking about, but by this point in our relationship he was so pissed at me that he was LOOKING for a reason to start a fight. He wanted me to go to one of the hospital departments and pick up a new deliver slip right away…so I started off to the stockroom to get a blank slip (typical since we always carried blank slips with us in case the department ran out)…he shouted at me "Where the hell do you think you're going??!!" I tried to explain to him that I needed to bring a slip with me, and he SCREAMED at me to "…just do what I told you to do and right NOW!!!" He was standing to the side of the hallway behind an empty cart and I needed to push my cart to the same side of the hallway to get it out of center of the hall…and that's when I made a BIG mistake…I shoved my cart towards the wall, it slammed into the cart that the old man was standing behind, which ricocheted and caught the old man square in the genitals…!! He doubled over in pain, so badly that he couldn't even speak let alone yell at me anymore…I remember muttering a "sorry about that" under my breath as I sped off to the department that had the supply order to be picked up…but all the way there I just KNEW my hours were numbered. When I got back to the stock room I didn't even give my boss a chance to fire me…I simply walked into his office, admitted what I did and the fact that I knew I was probably fired, and I quit on the spot. Like I said…my troubles had just started…!

My time in the air force was quiet and largely uneventful and although I didn't know it at the time it did include the last sexual relationship I would have with a woman for a VERY long time. I met my last girlfriend during that time, in 1989, and she left me 3 years later…from 1992 until this day, not only have I not had a social relationship with anyone, I have not had a PHYSICAL relationship with anyone…and that was 20 years ago…(more on that later in this chapter)! I shared a house with an old high school friend which was about 7 miles away from the airport where I worked, so for a good part of the year that I worked for the air force I walked and/or jogged to work. Even though my eating habits were catching up to me, the exercise I got during my year in the air force kept me pretty lean. I had gained about 40 pounds during my stock room days…from May of 1987 to about November of the same year…that's 40 pounds in only six months…!! I was able to lose most of that during my last year of service…the unit I worked for had a scale in its workroom and every morning when I got to work I would weigh myself before changing into my uniform, and the last time I ever remember weighing less than 200 pounds it was during my last days at the airport…I weighed 197 pounds and it was late 1987…and that was the LAST time I saw the underside of 200 pounds.

Since then my life has been a series of lies, rationalizations, diets, and eating disorders. Like so many of us, I suffer from an uncontrollable urge to eat…apart from motorcycle riding, sex, teaching, and writing, it is the one thing I enjoy doing the most. I don't suffer from a penchant or desire for any single voodoo food group…I am not a candy lover, or a carbohydrate junkie, or drink gallons of sugary soft drinks a day. No, my problem is more a "portion control" issue: I know what I should eat, I eat what I should eat (most of the time), but I just eat too MUCH of it…!! Take vegetables for example: I LOVE veggies, not as much as I love steak or pasta, but I do love 'em. For example, one of my favorite current delicacies is a dish from a local Chinese restaurant: broccoli in garlic sauce. It's a nice alternative from the meat-filled Chino-American dishes offered by so many Americanized Chinese restaurants, so every once in a while I order the dinner sized portion…enough broccoli for 2 or maybe 3 people. I will eat it ALL in a single sitting…a habit I picked up when I was in college, except now I am not burning off 5000 calories a day. I justify the session to myself the same way so many obese people do: I simply tell myself that it's OK because it was green vegetables and they're supposed to be good for me…and didn't I read somewhere that most diets allow you to eat as MUCH green vegetables as you want?

My main problem is this…and maybe some of you reading this book can relate to this condition: **I simply LOSE MY MIND WHEN IT COMES TO EATING**! I know what I am supposed to eat…I know HOW MUCH I should be eating to lose, or maintain…I know WHEN I should eat and how often…but when it comes to ordering food, cooking food, serving food, EATING food, and storing food…I lose my mind. **It's almost like I go into a food-induced trance**…I go unconscious for a while. Take a simple example: ordering Italian food from a restaurant that delivers. I look at the menu and I know I should order a small salad with a diet dressing…but when it comes time to speak on the phone those words don't come out of my mouth. Instead, I order things that I shouldn't be eating BUT COULD EAT if I was able to do so in moderation. So even though I feel guilty after placing the order, I can RATIONALIZE the order to myself psychologically by telling myself "well, as long as I only eat a small portion of what I ordered and save the rest for another time, I'll be OK."

OK…so the food comes and I put it in front of myself. Now what I SHOULD do is put the food in the kitchen and put that small portion I am visualizing in my mind on the plate and bring that to the table…but I lose my mind again. "That's too much trouble…" I tell myself, and "…I'll just bring ALL of the food into the living room, eat what I should eat, and then stop." Of course you can guess what happens…by the time I am finished I have eaten enough for 2 or 3 people (admittedly not nearly the Italian feasts from my Mama Brava's days, but still enough food for a small family) and I feel horribly guilty and miserable. There usually aren't enough leftovers to bother storing…so I usually wait a few hours and then, after the guilt has worn off, consume the leftovers and tell myself that they weren't worth storing (rationale #1)…and mom and dad taught me NOT to throw food away (#2)...and I will start a REAL diet tomorrow (#3)…and I have been doing that for 25 years now.

I am the self-appointed KING of rationalizations…making perfect and logical sense of every diet mistake that I make. My favorite one is of course the "…I'll start tomorrow…" rationalization, but there are so many…here are my Top-12 dieter's rationalizations, in no particular order, each one I have used extensively in the past. See how many YOU recognize:

1. The veggie rationale (discussed above): you can eat as many and as much as you want…forget that they might be drenched in fatty cream sauces, covered in cheese, or swimming in the oil you used to stir fry them!

2. Tomorrow is another day (ditto above): I'll start my diet tomorrow

3. Small portions of leftovers? Why bother storing them? It's not even big enough to qualify as a hors de oeuvre…! (last ditto)

4. Same price…same calories (discussed further in the chapter on societal contributions)

5. It's lean protein…I can have as much as I want (similar to the veggie rationale)

6. Pizza is bread (the dough), veggies (the sauce and any veggie toppings you may use), dairy (the cheese), and protein (because I always include pepperoni or beef or sausage on my pizza)…that's all four food groups…so where's the harm?

7. Do NOT waste food…ever…and NEVER throw food away unless it has CLEARLY spoiled…!! Wasting or throwing food away is a sin (a very popular religious threat from my elders when I grew up…and it stuck!)

8. Eat what is put in front of you…you don't want to insult the hostess do you?

9. If I only eat once a day, it's OK no matter what I eat (a rationalization I picked up during my "carbohydrate addict's diet" days, also discussed more later)

10. ANYTHING you put on a salad is OK: chopped eggs, bacon, ham, grated cheese, oily croutons… and so is adding 2 cups of bleu cheese dressing…because it's going on a SALAD…and salads are healthy, right?!

11. I can eat anything I want, as long as my caloric intake is within the dietary restrictions (aka the candy bar rationale…4 candy bars @ 250 calories each is the same as eating 1000 calories of real food)…calories are calories…right?

12. …and let's NOT forget the most famous rationale…as stupid as it still sounds…diet soft drinks negate the calories of anything you eat while you drink them…!!

My entire eating-life since I left the air force has been a series of rationalizations…I can't remember a non-diet meal where I didn't use at least one of them to make myself feel better about eating something I shouldn't have or eating too much of something. Many of you probably think that some of the rationalizations in my list sound pretty silly…but let me ask you: do you have some that YOU use that I failed to list? Everyone who has an eating disorder uses one or more rationalization to justify their behavior…it's like your rationale and logical mind goes to sleep while your "eating" mind takes over…and you will listen to anything it tells you that makes you feel better about your behavior, no matter how silly it sounds before or after you eat.

A little bit more about power eating…my worst bad habit. If you remember from last chapter, power eating is what I call those times when I lose my mind and sit down to eat as much of something (or several something's) as I can in one sitting. Cheeseburgers, pizza, Italian food, Chinese food, chicken nuggets, friend chicken…you name it, I have had a power eating session with it. The habit goes back to my West Point days, where I started practicing…but I perfected it during my four years in the army. I remember a friend of mine, a fellow alum from West point who graduated a year behind me…we met at Fort Hood during my last 15 months in the army. One of our favorite things to do was to go to this hamburger chain in Killeen Texas, outside of the base, called Whataburger…they had this special they ran…39 cent hamburgers and 49 cent cheeseburgers…absolute POISON and DISASTER for me…and my friend and I used to hit Whataburger at least once a week and buy burgers by the sackful…I can remember buying 10, 20, sometimes even 30 burgers at a time…we'd eat as many as we could in the restaurant and bring the rest back home to our apartments…where I would devour the rest over the period of an afternoon.

That segues nicely to another eating disorder I suffer from: what I like to call "closet eating." You've heard of closet drinkers: folks with drinking problems who never drink in public…they do all of their drinking alone behind closed and private doors. In later chapters I will talk about how uncomfortable it is for a fat person to eat anything in public…and it is that anxiety and embarrassment that drives us indoors as closet eaters. Let me give you a few examples of closet eating. My favorite practice of this disorder is when I eat out with family or friends. I would go to a diner or restaurant with friends and I would feel the eyes on me…I would feel that my friends and sometimes even the other patrons were staring at me, watching what I order, what I eat, how much I eat. I felt they were staring at me to see how a fat person eats…what I call the fishbowl effect (also described later in this book). Being the stubborn person that I am, I just couldn't give them that satisfaction…I simply would NOT be a performing seal for them…so I would falsely order some small portion of something…like for breakfast an egg white omelet, no starch, no meat, dry toast. Lunch would consist of a tuna sandwich, maybe some coleslaw and applesauce. Now, to be honest I will admit that for breakfast I WANTED to order cream chipped beef on toast, three fried eggs on top, a short stack of pancakes on the side, home fries with onions, maybe another meat like a double order of bacon, and coffee. For lunch I wanted a triple-decker club sandwich, chips and coleslaw (dieting or not, I love coleslaw), a side order of onion rings or fries, and diet soda (rationalization #11 strikes again…!). But that's exactly what everyone EXPECTS a fat person to order…and I wouldn't satisfy their freakish curiosity…so I would disappointment them and order something that a dieting fat person would order. To top it all off, I would only eat HALF of whatever I ordered and take the rest home…!! In my mind I was sending all of the assholes who were hoping to see a fat guy gorge himself so they could have a story to tell their friends…something like "…you shoulda seen this fat guy in the diner today…he ate enough food to feed a small African country all by himself…!"…I was sending them home shaking their heads, wondering "…how did that guy get so fat eating that way?" Of course that was all in my mind probably…MAYBE some of the people I have encountered along the way exhibited some perverse curiosity about my eating habits, but in my rational mind I know deep down inside that I probably never sent anyone home disappointed.

Where the closet eating disorder comes into play is AFTER the dining out experience…invariably I would stop somewhere on the way home and order from a drive-through…a sack of burgers, sandwiches, chicken…some fast food…and I would proceed home to eat by myself. I think the only ones I MIGHT have fooled were my friends..I think on more than one occasion I sent them home wondering why I wasn't losing any weight eating the way I was…but then again, maybe (probably) I am not giving my family and friends enough credit for intelligence. They would have to be complete morons to not see what is really going on, and they are certainly NOT morons.

Take past Holidays for example…another favorite closet eating opportunity for me. Same scenario: the family member doing the cooking would put out the right kinds of food for me in addition to the typical BAD Holiday foods…they would make sure there was a salad, light dressing, 2 or 3 veggies…and I would load my plate with small portions of the RIGHT STUFF…nibble a little bit here and there…and put on this HUGE martyr scene about how hard it is to diet during the holidays…and then I would stop at a store on the way home…except Christmas, when the stores are closed…so on Christmas I would make sure I had leftovers from the night before ready to be warmed up…but on all OTHER Holidays I would stop at a 24-hour convenience store on the way home and buy something to eat by myself.

I also suffer from urges, almost like those that I hear pregnant women have. I know what I should eat and usually I stick to that (too much of it, but good food nonetheless), but occasionally I get an urge for something bad that I just can't resist. These urges are so incredibly intense that often I will make a special trip out of the house to get my "fix." You have to understand, ever since I became mostly housebound (more on that later) I will try everything I can to avoid leaving the house. My housebound status is completely self-inflicted; luckily I can still get around under my own power and I can still drive my truck with increasing difficulty, but I am still ambulatory…the medical term for being "mobile." So I will order cooked food from places that deliver, I patronize companies that deliver packaged food to the home, I order a lot from websites like Amazon and wholesalers…and if one of the major supermarket chains ever offers a grocery delivery service in my area, I will be one of their best customers. However…when I get to "jonesin" for some TastyKakes, a fresh hoagie, a certain kind of candy bar, or just simply a dozen donuts…I just have to have them…and I will leave the sanctuary of my home just to get them.

Back to my largely boring historical struggle with food. During my year in the air force I met the woman who became my LAST serious social relationship and who may ALSO be…sadly, the last sexual relationship I will ever have. We met through mutual friends and developed a king of love-hate relationship; as most relationships do, it started intensely and was wonderful for a while, but things began to deteriorate when I lost my air force job and entered the private sector. The rest of the details behind that relationship are of no consequence to the overall purpose of this book, but certain aspects of it were influential to my ultimate downward spiral, so I think they deserve mention here. As our relationship soured I realized that there were only a few activities during which we actually got along. One of them was sex of course, but as the relationship deteriorated even that had become had become infrequent and unsatisfying…but while we were engaged in "it"…at least we weren't fighting. But the one activity during which we were at complete and total peace with each other was when we were EATING…! We would fight incessantly…about everything…but when we were eating, gorging ourselves…there was blissful silence and harmony…! The funny thing is we both were overweight when we met and were VERY overweight when we split up…so you would THINK that we would be in agreement about dieting. You would expect two people like us to support each other in our efforts to lose weight and become healthier, but we even argued about dieting and eating..!! She was, for lack of a better analogy, passionate about eating…and she HATED to do anything alone…! When she was trying to diet she was INTENSE about the diet…and I had NO choice but to go along for the ride…there would be no cheating in our house, we would avoid scenarios when we would be tempted by food, she would measure everything on a food scale…and of course harassing me about what I ate and when. However, when she was NOT dieting, she was equally intense…and equally averse to doing it alone! She would eat whatever she wanted, whenever she wanted…and she would expect me to go along with her. I tried more often than she did to lose weight…we both went on NutriSystem together…on two separate occasions if I recall correctly…but whenever she got discouraged and gave up…also known as "the rest of the time"…she just ate when she wanted to eat…and during those times when she was eating and I was still trying to diet she made my life a living hell…! Some of the most monumental fights we had involved eating…she wanted to and I did not. She would come home from work and would suggest that we order from the local pizzeria (owned and operated by a classmate from my high school days)…this would happen 3 or 4 days a week since during the week when we worked neither of us felt much like cooking after a long day. If I had the nerve to admit that I was trying to watch what I ate…or was trying to lose a few pounds…she would start in with the "…so what am I supposed to do? Eat alone?!" She would NEVER order food for herself unless there was something in the order for me…she would sulk, pout, and look for reasons to argue with me…she would complain about having hunger headaches or be sick to her stomach…and to each argument I offered the simple defense: THEN JUST GO AHEAD AND EAT

DAMMIT…! But since eating alone was out of the question and not an option for her, she would harass me relentlessly for hours until I gave in and ordered some food. I usually TRIED to get away with ordering a salad, and that worked sometimes…if her pre-order tantrum was especially drawn out, she would feel pretty lucky to have me order anything at all, so on those occasions she wouldn't care what I ordered. However, that lasted only a short while…she started to complain that a salad was not REAL food and that if I wasn't going to order anything real, then she wouldn't order anything at all…and the pre-order harassment would start all over again until I agreed to order something substantial…!

One day I decided to try something…I stopped at the pizzeria and spoke to my friend and arranged a trick: I set it up with him and his staff…especially those who took orders from the phone…that whenever I called an order in they were to delete the second item from the order. I set up a password phrase for his staff to key on…when I called and used the password, they were to simply delete the second item from the order…! It worked like a charm for a while…my girlfriend had NO idea what was going on...! She would come home from work and on those days when she asked to order food from the pizzeria I would immediately agree…just that simple act avoided HOURS of grief for me…! Since I was the one who always called the orders in, it was easy: I would call the order in, and when the person answered the phone, I would use my password phrase…something like "Is the lasagna fresh this week?" Everyone in the pizzeria knew who I was and what was going on…hell it even became fun for them, kinda like a little game and we enjoyed it for a while. I changed the password phrase every week or two…asking every day about the freshness of the lasagna would only fool her for so long. Sometimes I would order something HUGE from the menu…like a whole pizza just for myself, knowing full well that whatever I ordered it would be deleted from the order. They would prepare my girlfriend's food and deliver it…but when we opened the bag to pass out the food…there would be nothing in the bag for me to eat. She would be FURIOUS when this happened…especially because it started happening so often…but she also hated to eat cold food, and she hated waiting even more…so when the food came without my part of the order I would tell her to just eat and I would make something for myself from whatever was in the fridge…which was usually nothing during the week. Sometimes, if I thought she was getting suspicious, to throw her off the scent I would actually order something like a salad and just not use the password phrase…so on those occasions my food would arrive with hers and that would alleviate any suspicions she would have…but only for a while. This trick worked for a few short months…finally she figured out what was going on (I don't remember HOW she figured it out…I just remember she did…!) and the game was over.

I tell this story because…well, because it's kinda funny and it always makes me laugh when I think about it…but also because it marks my last dying gasp at really trying to lose weight until just recently. After a while I must admit with more than just a little shame that I gave up really trying. By the time my last real girlfriend left me in early 1992, I was ruined: please note that I do NOT blame her, because even though we were "calorically incompatible" for each other (that's MY term for it…catchy aint it? I might copyright it..!), it was NOT her fault that I am the way I am today. After our break up there was a series of half-hearted failed attempts at losing weight (more on that in later chapters), but nothing that I was able to sustain long enough for it to take hold…no attempts that have resulted in what the experts (and me too) agree is the KEY to successful weight loss…not just weight loss but an entire lifestyle change. In the same amount of time, from 1992 to today, I was able to quit smoking cigarettes (2 pack a day smoker for 15 years, quit in 1994), I was able to quit drinking (I still enjoy the rare sip of champagne or wine on VERY special occasions, but mostly I am a tea-totaler), but food is the one vice that I cannot beat…it hasn't beat me yet, not until I am dead and in my grave…but it has taken control over me and I am still looking for that incentive that will allow me to turn things around.

That incentive ALMOST came a few years ago, and before I move on to discuss other issues regarding obesity in our society, I need to tell you about the day a toilet woke me up. From 1992 when my girlfriend left me until 1998, my weight didn't fluctuate very much. I was about 250 pounds in 1992 and while I would sometimes weigh as much as 270 or 280 lbs at my heaviest and maybe 235 at my lightest during those years, for the most part my weight hovered around 250 pounds. I was working for a consulting firm in south/central New Jersey at the time…the drive to work was only 45 minutes…on rural/suburban back roads, so what I would do was get to work VERY early in the morning…around 4 am…and I would walk for 2 hours every morning. I would shower before I left home and since walking would not cause me to break a sweat I could dress in my shorts or sweats to work and change into my business attire in my private office after my walk. Sometimes I would even walk for 45 minutes during lunch with a friend of mine…so 2 workouts x 5 days a week kept me reasonably fit and kept my weight level.

In 1998 things changed again, and again they changed for the worse. I took a job with another company out of state, and the daily commute was two hours a day, from doorstep to doorstep. For the first couple of years I was still living in New Jersey (I couldn't sell my house) and I had to commute every day. At first I tried to commute AND maintain my walking schedule, but that didn't work out too well…especially after the day when one of the company senior VPs caught me in my underwear…changing from my walking gear into my business clothes in my OPEN cubicle…but that's a story for another book…!

I had been working at my new job for about 5 years when it happened…I was assigned to assist a project we were managing for a big computer company in mid-state New York. My weight ballooned from 250 pounds to somewhere in the 300s by this time…maybe even close to 400 pounds. Now, for anyone who is morbidly obese like me, you already know the difficulties that arise from massive weight gain…so many of the simple, basic, human operations that most people take for granted become difficult and sometimes even impossible. Take toilet habits for example: for those of you who are unfamiliar with this phenomenon, when you gain a massive amount of weight there is a

LOT more "real estate" that you have to negotiate in order to "complete the transaction." In other (more graphic) words, when you get real fat it becomes VERY difficult to clean yourself…! Sorry for the unsavory image, but there it is…! This is not a phenomenon that occurs overnight…first it just becomes difficult to clean yourself: let's face it, since your arms are not growing longer to keep pace with your weight gain, there is MORE of you to stretch your arm across to get your hand to where it needs to be. Then as you gain more weight you have to STRAIN, and as your condition continues to deteriorate then you begin to look for ways to assist yourself in this endeavor…like using the stall walls as leverage to push against, or maybe shifting your weight on the toilet seat to use your legs to your advantage…it's not a tasty concept, but I have been there and it's just a fact of life.

Back to the project: we were given a small office complex to use while we worked for this client, and just outside our offices was a public men's toilet, very convenient. By this time in my weight gain I was using several of the techniques I described above when I went to the toilet: I would use my right hand to push against the wall/stall on my right side and I would shift myself closer to the front edge of the toilet so that I could use my legs to twist myself into the position I needed to be in to get the job done. The bathroom poses I used to strike in those days probably could have qualified me for a tryout as a member of Cirque de Soleil, but I had no choice. What I DIDN'T count on was the wall-mounted toilet.

As you know, most toilets sit on the floor…solid, stable…but there is a toilet that is designed to attach to the wall…it's called "cantilevering": when something is supported by the point where it attaches to the structure and then hangs out suspended in mid air…so the only thing holding these toilets up are whatever attachment system(s) the designer used plus the strength of the toilet itself. The toilets in our home office lavatory were floor mounted, and I honestly never gave any thought to the disaster that ultimately occurred at this client's office. I went to the bathroom one day, a day like any other…took care of my business and was completing the paperwork (as we all do)…I had to slide forward on the toilet seat, push to the left with my legs while simultaneously pushing against the stall wall on my right in order to STRAIN myself into position to get clean…and then disaster struck…!

I guess it could have been a combination of several things going wrong at the same time…a stress crack in a weak toilet maybe…too much weight suspended too far forward on the toilet itself maybe…wall anchors that were not driven into the proper supporting structure maybe…the added stress of me pushing both to the left and right with my arm and legs…but one second I was sitting on the toilet and the next second I was sitting on the floor…SOAKED with toilet water up to the back of my shirt collar…! The toilet had experienced what they call in the construction business "catastrophic failure": it ripped itself from the wall and landed on the floor. Now before I get any emails asking me the obvious question…NO…I was lucky enough to have "pre-flushed" prior to the catastrophe…a courtesy I extend in most cases when I visit the lavatory…so all that was in the toilet when it broke was clean water and the remnants of the paperwork I had just completed. As if breaking a toilet was not bad enough (the noise could have woke the dead, but the doors were thick and well insulated), I was not alone in the lavatory when the accident occurred. There was another employee from my company in the stall to my right, and when he heard the noise he immediately asked me if I was OK (is it inappropriate to suggest that the noise might have "scared the shit out of him?"). I had recovered by then, was dressed (pulled my pants up), so I replied that everything was all right, that the toilet had broke but I was OK. He asked me if I was sure that I was OK…did I need any help…etc, etc, so I told him that he didn't need to wait around for me…I would take care of everything. I just didn't want to face this young guy…I had never been so embarrassed in my whole life…! When I heard him leave, I exited the stall and washed my hands quickly so I could get out of there before anyone else came in…but not fast enough it seemed…because my lavatory friend came back in with a friend of his own, carrying an "out of order" sign for the stall I was in (really, was that necessary? Did anyone seeing the destruction in that stall need a sign to tell them that toilet was out of order? Damn thing was sitting on the floor for crying out loud…!). So now the secret was out: two guys from my company knew that fat old Bill D had demolished a toilet in the customer's men's lavatory…and I knew it was only a matter of time before the jokes and snickers and whispers and sneers and side glances would begin. I immediately went into our senior project manager's office and confessed what I had done…I apologized and offered to pay for the damages…even offering to go to our customer and admit that I was the person who had destroyed their toilet…but the project manager had mercy on me and offered to approach our client himself. By the end of that day my worst fears were realized: people were coming up to me asking me if I had really demolished a toilet…what happened…was I ok…what did it sound like…what did the project manager say…what did the client say…etc, etc. Luckily for me that was the last day of that week that I was scheduled to be on site, so I was able to go home to New Jersey at the end of the day. Curiously enough I was notified a few days later that my services would no longer be needed at that project site…no surprise there…!! I was the butt of many company jokes for the remainder of my tenure with that company…I even made the project yearbook…a photo of the broken toilet, sadly sagging forward with an "out of order" sign attached to it…and the caption under the photo read "the toilet that Bill broke" with some miscellaneous snide remarks about me being a "toilet assassin" and about the toilet inspector failing to inspect that toilet for compression and weight testing. You can't imagine how proud I was…!

So from around 1993 when I destroyed the toilet to 1998 I just continued to grow. At my peak I weighed 568 pounds dressed, and all KINDS of medical problems began to crop up. Aside from the normal adverse side effects of obesity like high blood pressure, a liver disorder, borderline Type II diabetes, and circulatory problems, I developed what the medical profession calls a "panus." You see, I got so fat that I couldn't sleep lying down…so I started to sleep sitting up in a chair. It was more comfortable, but the weight of my stomach sitting in my lap blocked my lymph system, that's the system that carries excess fluid and fatty tissue to your drainage system so your body can rid itself of waste material. If your body can't expel the excess fluid and tissue, it will be stored somewhere in your body. Obese people know this, but most non-obese people may not: not all obese people store this weight in the same place(s) on their bodies. Some get big stomachs, some get big butts, some retain fat on their arms or legs. Since I was blocking my lymph system at the waist, all excess fluid and tissue from below my waist was being retained…so one of the areas where I retained a substantial amount of fat was in a fat roll over my pubic area. As it was described to me this physiological condition is known as paniculitis…and the treatment is surgery…a massive tummy tuck called a paniculectomy. My panus was categorized as a stage 5: the bigger the number the bigger the panus. Stage 5 is the most severe stage, and in my case it meant that my panus was hanging down below my knees. At the time of my surgery it weighed in excess of 50 lbs.

So in March of 2007 I went in for body reconstruction surgery to remove the panus. It was a relatively painless and quick operation: 2 hours later I was a miraculous 53 pounds lighter…! My scar went from hip to hip but I felt great…the only way to describe my relief is to get you to imagine that you have a basketball filled with water hanging in front of your legs…imagine trying to walk, drive a car, sit down properly, and dress yourself in normal clothes. It was painful, humiliating, inconvenient, and embarrassing…there was just no way to hide something that big no matter what I did. Yet, in less than 2 hours, the basketball was excised from my body and I was 53 pounds lighter…like a miracle.

I'll spare you the boring details of what has transpired from then to now…as of the summer of 2012, the condition has recurred…only not in the same place. Since I still had to sleep in an upright position immediately following the surgery (yes, I know…"why don't I just stop sleeping sitting up?"…long story there too) and my lymph system was still mostly blocked, my body started to store tissue again only 2 weeks after my 2007 surgery. This time, however, my body chose my scrotum (yes, you read that correctly) to store this waste tissue and fluid. As of the writing of this book, my scrotum has swollen to the size of a medium pumpkin and it weighs somewhere in the vicinity of 45 pounds. All of the issues I listed above that I suffered from with the panus I am suffering from now, only it's worse. Instead of having that "water filled basketball" in FRONT of my legs, I now have one BETWEEN my legs…! I am living on a federal disability pension from the social security administration and I cannot work…at least not full-time. I am hoping that I will qualify for another surgery as soon as I lose enough weight to reduce the danger to me going under anesthesia, but until then I am continuing to try to manage my appetite, watching my portion size, and avoiding the public eye as much as possible…!

Chapter 3: Diets (I've been on most of 'em), surgical solutions, and going to jail (a funny story about Nutrisystem freeze dried burgers)

Like most dieters, I have been on almost every commercial diet out there. Most of them showed promise, and some even resulted in limited (albeit short-term) success ranging from a couple of pounds up to double-digit losses. Some, however, were just plain ridiculous, but I tried 'em anyway…! Here are the ones I can remember…I'm sure there are others, but my memory of them must have been wiped out due to cerebral malnutrition…in other words my friggin brain was so starved by a lack of calories that it caused me to lose all recollection of them…!

By the way, while I will make no claims…good OR bad…regarding the medical or nutritional benefits of any of these diets, it should be stated here that oh-so-popular disclaimer we fat people hear all of the time, and that is: *you should NEVER start any diet without first consulting with your doctor AND including the expertise of a licensed nutritionist in your diet efforts*. Also, while I didn't have very much success with any of them in their purest forms, they are all effective in their own right and can probably lay claim to their own significant number of success stories. The blame for why these diets did not work for me is MINE…not the diet's…they were just not the right fixes for me.

NutriSystem (let's just call it NS): This diet became very popular back in the late 1980s. When it first came out it seemed to be a diet for the elite…membership cost a LOT of money PLUS it cost a lot of money for their food…and you could only get their food as a member. The program included weekly weigh-ins much like Weight Watchers, group discussion sessions, and personal nutritionist/exercise counseling.

The single characteristic I dislike most about NS is the fact that almost ALL of your fruits and vegetables have to be bought separately, including some other fresh items like dairy, breads and rolls, and eggs. For someone like me who has trouble avoiding "bad" foods when they go shopping, NS is not a good option. Also, since most of your vegetables are supposed to be bought fresh and cooked, anyone who has trouble with portion control may find it difficult to lose significant amounts of weight on NS. In fact, if you are like me…someone who rationalizes that "…fruits and veggies are good for me, therefore I can have as much as I want…", you might be able to cut way back on your portions of entrees, but you will make up for that deficit with an equal number OR MORE calories in "innocent looking" things like potatoes, sweet fruits, and salads with fatty dressing.

I have tried NS several times in the past 20 years. The first time I tried NS was in 1990 when my girlfriend and I wanted to lose some weight…yes, the same woman that I discussed in some detail in the last chapter. We were both quite sporty and fit when we met…she was 5'7" and weighed somewhere around 135 pounds…and looked VERY nice for her frame and height…and I weighed about 219 pounds…ALSO not TOO bad for my height…! Because our favorite thing to do together was eat, from 1988 when we met until our first try with NS we had ballooned up nicely: she weighed about 175 pounds and I topped out at about 275. We did OK on the diet, but then we started to lose our minds. Our ultimate downfall was due largely to a concoction she would make that consisted of potatoes, onions, and peppers. Like I said, NS requires you to prepare your own vegetables and side dishes…and this was one way we could get our starches and veggies together. She would chop the ingredients into large chunks, microwave them to get them soft, and then fry them in some non-stick cooking spray like Pam to crisp them up. Initially we had some great success with this side dish and it became a staple in our diets. We would use 3 potatoes, a whole onion and a whole bell pepper in the recipe. For several weeks we lost a steady amount of weight.

But like so many failed attempts at dieting, our calorie-starved minds started the rationalization process: a medium potato only has about 70 calories…and the calories in an onion and a pepper are negligible. Why then can't we INCREASE the amount of this stuff that we eat? The recipe went from 4, then to 5, then to 6, and finally to SEVEN large baking potatoes…and 2 each whole large yellow onions and green peppers. We also started to add small amounts of cooking oil to enhance the taste of the results because…stand-by for another rationalization…hey, a few tablespoons of vegetable oil can't hurt, can they?

Our weight loss slowed, then stopped…and we couldn't understand why. We did the math: 7 potatoes x 70 calories each is only about 500 calories…add another 200 calories MAX for the onions and peppers and that's only 700 calories…divided by 2 (we would split what we made equally between us) that's only 350 calories each. If we are trying to get 1500 calories a day, and our NS food only gives us 1000, we're still OK, aren't we?

Of course we failed to consider the size of the potatoes…the monster baking potatoes we were using at the end were probably twice the number of cals as a "medium potato." Adding a significant number of calories from the oil, it's no wonder we stopped losing weight. After about 3 or 4 weeks of not losing any weight, we gave up.

I've been on and off NS several times since then, especially since they started offering their food online. Generally I like their food…it's convenient and tastes good, it travels well (most of it is freeze dried or vacuum sealed, needing no refrigeration) and it doesn't take up too much room. The portion sizes are too small, but no smaller than any other brand. The convenience however is offset by the fact that you STILL have to supplement the diet with fresh products. I have found NS to be a better diet for when I want to MAINTAIN a specific weight…it's a good transitional or "bridge" diet that I can use when I am between other programs. However, I think the reason I keep coming back to NS is because Marie Osmond has been their spokesperson for some time now and I have had a crush on Marie ever since she recorded her first record at the age of 13. I was 12 and COMPLETELY in love, and I never got over it. I think that subconsciously in the back of my mind I am hoping that one day I'll lose enough weight on NS that I will be invited by the company to do an infomercial with Marie…!

Jenny Craig: Not much to say about Jenny…tried it and found it about as effective as NS…except that the food is not as available in my area. Valerie Bertinelli, who was Jenny's spokesperson, was my OTHER crush in high school…any wonder why I tried Jenny?

Weight Watchers: been on it several times, don't like it. I know it has been successful for a LOT of people, but I never liked the public weigh-ins. I have had people tell me that the weigh-ins are no longer mandatory, and I get lectures that …"everyone at the weigh-in is in the same boat I am in, so why am I embarrassed?…but I'm not buying any of it. I do like their food…I buy a lot of it in the supermarket. For frozen diet food, it's not bad.

Richard Simmons Deal-a-Meal: I thought this diet was cool when he first introduced it to the public…a system of cards that represent servings of the four food groups plus fats. You got serving cards, this neat plastic folder to hold your cards in, a book that converted popular foods into "servings" by weight and volume, some motivational listening material on cassette (cassettes; that should give you some indication how long ago it was that I was on Deal-a-meal) and some fill-in-the-blanks progress sheets to track your loss. You would determine how many calories you were supposed to have each day by considering your sex, your weight, your lifestyle, and how much you wanted to lose…then the plan would tell you how many servings of each food group you were allowed each day. You would count out the appropriate number of cards for your servings, and place them on one side of your folder. As you ate your food during the day you would move the cards from "how much I can eat" side of the folder to the "how much I ate today" side of the folder. Once all of your cards were moved over, you were done eating for the day.

How can anyone fail with a system that is so simple? Easy…when you start rationalizing with simple and somewhat reasonable things like the "calories are calories" argument: "why can't I substitute 3 veggie cards for 2 fruit cards…the calories are the same…" or "aren't 500 calories of fruit the same as 500 calories of bread?" I would try some really ridiculous substitutions…like substituting fruits and vegetables for more meat, or more fat. Deal-a-Meal is probably the only diet where a psycho like me can rationalize that "bacon is the same as broccoli"…! At the end I was simply cheating the system…adding extra servings of almost everything except vegetables.

The Pritikin Principle: The only diet I was on with a name that sounded more like a science lesson than a diet. Wasn't on this one very long, only a few weeks…memories of a LOT of beans-with-the-accompanying-flatulence, brown rice, green and stringy vegetables, high fiber…and did I mention a lot of farting? Of course my attempt at the Pritikin Principle morphed into more cheating and rationalizing…and cartons upon cartons of red beans and rice from Popeye's chicken. Hey, foods that are low in fat and fill you up quickly…so red beans and rice should qualify…right?

Atkins: The pinnacle of low-carb, low-fat, high protein diets. Unlike the carbohydrate addicts diet described below (similar principle to Atkins but different), Atkins severely restricts your carb intake…it stresses "good" carbs, but Dr. Atkins' definition of "good" certainly did NOT mean good tasting…! Got tired of the lack of tasty carbs quickly…no potatoes, no pasta, no processed breads or rolls…just tons of brown rice and whole grains…YUK…! But in his defense, the Atkins diet sure did make me regular.

South Beach: Two whole weeks of NO STARCHES…no pasta, potatoes, rice, or baked goods of any kind…just complex carbohydrate veggies and low-fat lean proteins….THAT'S what marked the beginning AND THE END of this diet for me…never made it past the "cleansing period."

The Zone: Now THIS diet I was able to get behind…at least at first. While it stressed low-fat, low-simple carbs, and high protein, it still allowed all of those categories in small controlled doses. What torpedoed this diet for me was the eating schedule: you are supposed to eat a "zone" meal within an hour of getting up in the am (before I have even had my coffee or my digestive system is awake) AND you are supposed to eat FIVE TIMES a day…! Considering my poor track record with portion control, any diet that has me sitting at the meal table 5 times a day is doomed to failure.

What really ruined the zone diet for me was the food…I ordered frozen zone meals from a local prepared food company in my area, and the food was just not my taste…the best way I can describe it is to say that the chef "tried too hard." They tried to "gourmet up" the food too much rather than keeping it simple…my amateur palate is just not accustomed to that diversity. That one lasted about 2 months.

Grapefruit: Yes, I tried it…and anyone else who has probably thinks the same thing I do: that the person who developed it must have been in a mental institution. Within a week I had such bad heartburn from the gallons of acid I was getting from the fruit that I was popping Rolaids like they were candy…and since they were not the sugar-free Rolaids, the weight I was losing eating grapefruit was offset by what I was gaining in the Rolaids…!

Egg: Like the beans on Pritikin, eggs give me gas…really bad, sulfuric-rotten, uncontrollable gas, the kind that can clear a room within minutes. Need I say more?

Oh yeah, there is that cholesterol thing too….it's a shame, I really like eggs in every form, and I was actually losing weight for a while…it was just that nobody could stand being around me for long…!

Cabbage Soup: I never should have used the recipe that called for massive amounts of cayenne pepper…this time, instead of burning when it went in like the grapefruit diet, it burned coming out…! To anyone considering this diet, it is an unhealthy and VERY temporary way to lose a few pounds…it worked for me in cleansing my system, but the weight came back on within days of my "1 week period."

The Cookie diet: For those of you who are not familiar with this one, don't get too excited…it's not a diet that allows you to ingest an entire package of Oreo Double Stuff's at a sitting…! No, some experts somewhere developed a recipe for a "cookie" that is supposed to be eaten in place of 2 meals a day…you eat 6 "special recipe" cookies a day, which amounts to about 500 calories, and then you eat a sensible dinner. However, that term "sensible" is vague and ambiguous…to me, sensible means making sure I get my side order of meatballs with extra sauce to make sure I get my vegetables…! The cookie diet FORBIDS red meat, fruits, and dairy of any kind…AND no other carbohydrates at all…!

I lasted about 3 days on the cookie diet…when I started eating all six cookies at a time with my coffee in the morning I knew it was time to move on…!

Medifast: I have only been on two supplement diets in my life, and this is one of them. Supplements 5 times a day in the form of bars, shakes, soups, hot and cold beverages, and even scrambled eggs, and then that "sensible dinner" I have so much trouble with. This one lasted about 4 months…not bad for me, but it's because I was in training for bariatric surgery that I HOPED a Johns Hopkins surgeon was going to perform…neither the diet nor the surgeon worked out for me…!

Supplement diets don't work for me at all…I need real food, even if it's only a mouthful.

Slimfast: The OTHER supplement diet I tried. I did the wet shakes in cans, the dry powder in cans…add water or skim milk and shake well…and the candy bars. Slimfast is good for me as a snack in between meals when I am maintaining, but no good if I am trying to lose.

The Subway Jared diet: Was pretty desperate by the time Jared came on the scene…can you believe ANY fast-food company that makes hoagies (in your neck of the woods you may call them sandwiches, subs, grinders, or torpedoes) promoting a diet composed entirely of their food as an acceptable substitute for a healthy menu? Well I fell for it…was eating those Subway 12" veggies twice a day…lettuce, tomato, onion, and pickles with brown mustard only please…until I was sick of looking at them. Even had some success for a while too…but then black olives, high in fat, made it onto my veggies…then some Dijon…then some mayonnaise…then a couple of slices of cheese…and finally why not a slice or two of low-fat roast beef or ham or turkey? You can see where this is going, can't you?

Lean Cuisine, Healthy Choice: By far the diet food(s) with which I have had the most success. I like both varieties, they both include veggies and sometimes fruit (if you buy the full meal varieties), they are reasonably filling, and if you check the nutritional panels you can pick varieties that are low sodium (if you have high blood pressure like me), low carb, and low sugar (for you borderline Type II's out there). What's also great about them is they are easy to store, easy to prepare (from frozen to hot in about 6 minutes tops), and when you are crazy hungry you can eat two of them at a sitting without cheating too much…because there are some varieties that are less than 300 calories, which is minimal. The only drawback is that they don't travel well, but all you have to do when you're on the road is find a supermarket…! If I was ranking these diet plans on a 5-star scale, these meals would be the only ones to score over a 4 out of 5 stars.

The Carbohydrate Addicts Diet: I saved this one for last because in my opinion it was, without exception, the most ridiculous diet ever developed…and I don't care if anyone wants to sue me for saying that…! It's a lot like the other carb-hating diets I tried (and listed above): it proposes a high-lean-protein diet with less carbs. You basically eat reasonable quantities of lean protein and non-starchy veggies twice a day, NO CARBS…but in this case, the diet has one overwhelmingly unique characteristic with regards to that "sensible" third meal: <u>you can eat as much as you want of whatever you want for one hour a day</u>…!

I actually bought the book on this diet, because when it was explained to me by a friend many years ago I simply could NOT believe what I was being told. I could eat as much of anything I wanted for a whole hour? Ridiculous I thought…this quack doctor has NO IDEA who he is dealing with here…memories of my West Point days ran through my mind, and those good ole days of power eating, Mama Brava's, and mess hall raids. But I read the book and it started to make sense…the book described how your system learns to adapt to being starved for carbs…then it adjusts…and finally you just lose your craving for them. The doctor described how your all-you-can-eat meal during the first couple of days on the diet would be carb-heavy, but within a week or two you should find yourself eliminating carbs from your meal completely. The "free meal" rules were as follows:

1. You could eat anything…including carbs…and as much as you wanted

2. The meal was to last only ONE contiguous, uninterrupted hour…no eating for 15 minutes, waiting 2 hours, and then eating for 45 minutes later. But you could eat in the first 5 minutes of that hour and the last 5 minutes of that hour if you chose.

The doctor also described how your eating pattern would change during your free meal. He suggested that you would eat for most of the whole hour of your free meal at first, but as your stomach shrunk (a phenomenon that has yet to ever occur in my system…maybe my stomach is made of something that is not elastic..?) you would find yourself getting full in 30 minutes, then 20, then 15, and then 10 minutes. Before too long you would eat freely for about 5 minutes before getting full, and then stop.

So I tried it, and low and behold the doctor was right: at first I loaded up heavy on the carbs during my free meal…buckets of potatoes, French fries, cakes and pies…AND I ate for the whole hour, but soon I lost my taste for the carb heavy meals and transitioned to something a bit more reasonable. The weight was coming off slowly, I was eating everything I wanted once a day, which was OK with me, and the rest of the day was easy enough to endure.

Well, as the philosophers say, if it looks too good to be true, then it probably is…and the carb addict's diet was too good to be true. My system adjusted to the diet and those old cravings came back with a vengeance. In addition the weight loss was only temporary...at first it slowed, then it stopped, and then I started to put the weight back on. My free meal DID shorten to 5 minutes, but within a month it was back to 60 minutes...and the quantities of food I was putting down were incredible…! Boxes of TastyKakes, whole pies, 2 large baked potatoes at a time loaded with butter and sour cream, buckets of the Colonel's chicken, and sackfuls of cheeseburgers…it was like being back in college…! I was FURIOUS…! I did everything right, I followed the diet to the letter…why was I not losing weight?

There was a section in the book written for guys like me: if you found yourself not losing weight on the diet, there were some troubleshooting rules to follow:

1. First, consume a large salad BEFORE eating your free meal…this was intended, clearly, to fill you up before your buffet…but what the doctor didn't know was that I liked my salads with an entire jar of Marie's Chunky Bleu Cheese dressing, some bacon, cheese, croutons, and some cooked chicken on top. Not what he had in mind I am sure….

2. If #1 didn't work, which it didn't for me…his next suggestion was to drink a 16 oz. glass of water before the salad and the buffet.

Well, that's when I gave up on that diet…if I have to drink 16 ounces of water AND eat a big dry salad every day before eating my one meal of the day, then the diet has some serious flaws in it. But it was fun while it lasted…I still have sweet dreams about those "all you can eat in 60 minute" meals.

Fat camps: Although I have never taken advantage of this type of diet program I have always felt that the format and execution of the program would be perfect for me, if only such programs were within the income range of someone on a disability pension; their drawback is that they are prohibitively expensive.

The premise is that you relocate to a sight and live there for an extended period of time…I have heard of programs lasting 6 months and some even longer, but I'm sure that if your money is good and your checkbook holds out the facility will accommodate your needs if you feel an extended visit is required. You live at the facility and eat only what they provide you…but this is where the facilities deviate from the form. The best facilities are remotely located and the patients have no access to transportation so that you cannot "cheat" by ordering Domino's pizza delivered every night. You eat a strictly proportioned menu specifically formulated for your sex, age, metabolism, health, and the amount of weight you want to lose. There are individual and/or group therapy sessions that cover the psychological aspect of eating disorders, which are also intended to ease your ultimate transition back into normal eating society upon completion. Of course exercise is an essential part of the program, also intended to facilitate your reintroduction into a normal life and to teach you the importance of living a complete healthy lifestyle and not JUST a diet. Other qualities I have heard the BEST programs possess are mail inspections so that no foreign food can be sent to you through UPS or FedEx, family visitations by appointment and prescheduled so that you can show off your progress to loved ones (and some programs even SEARCH your loved ones before entering the facility to ensure, again, no cheating occurs), and even a graduation ceremony. Yup, if these programs were within my financial grasp I would be writing this book from there right now…I just can't afford it.

Surgery: Bariatric surgery in all of its forms is up 40% in the past few years…typical American solution for a problem, treat the disease AFTER it has become an epidemic rather than treating the cause at the source. That old "ounce of prevention is worth a pound of cure" philosophy would have come in handy about 20 years ago when we all started to get fat.

I researched ALL of the most popular bariatric surgeries including several plastic surgery solutions. There are new procedures being introduced every day, but the three most popular are as follows:

Stomach banding: This is the surgery I had in December of 2009, and it has been reasonably successful for me. It can be done laparoscopic-ally (the one I chose) with minimal incisions into your stomach cavity or it can be done via regular full-incision surgery. It consists of a band installed around the top of your stomach, forming a small pouch at the top of your stomach. When you eat, the food fills up this small pouch making you feel fuller faster, thereby resulting in eating smaller meals. Of course as you lose weight the band loosens, which will cause the food to flow freely again, but your surgeon can tighten the band without additional surgery simply by injecting saline solution into a port that is left just under the surface of your skin during surgery. When the saline is injected, it fills a bladder on the inside of your band, thereby tightening the band and the hole again…and you start again from the beginning.

This surgery requires a lot less recuperation time and has less potential adverse side effects or possible complications…a BIG selling point for me. It is also reversible…in the event the band causes me additional physiological complications I can simply have it removed in the future. It is also the only surgery where you can have one of the more delicate surgeries listed below performed after the banding surgery.

Gastric bypass: Also known as Roux-en-Y and (in some circles) the duodenal switch, the surgeon cuts your small intestine from its original location at the bottom of your stomach and bypasses a significant portion of the intestine…reattaching it closer to where the small intestine feeds into the large intestine. Since the small intestine is where most of our food is absorbed…if the small intestine is bypassed and the absorption process is decreased, then less food will be absorbed and you will lose weight. This surgery can now also be done laparoscopically or via full incision. There is a LAUNDRY list of rules and restrictions attached to this surgery, but it does hold the distinction of being the most effective surgery, with very substantial success rates and significant weight losses. It is also the "quickest" weight loss solution…almost 40% faster than weight loss from banding surgery.

Stomach reduction: Also known as sleeve gastrectomy, its name says it all…the removal and stapling (or stitching) of a portion of the stomach. Once removed and sewn (stapled) back up, the stomach resembles a sort of "sleeve"; hence the term sleeve gastrectomy. There has been some research with a double procedure that combines the removal of a portion of the stomach, the closure of the remaining stomach, and then the installation of a band around the remaining stomach to avoid the possibility that the remaining stomach will stretch due to overeating.

Well, that's about it…let me close this chapter by sharing with you a story about diet food that almost got me shot and landed me in jail. It was 1993 and my former girlfriend was a year gone and I was on my own again. I re-joined Nutrisystem solo this time, and on Saturdays I would drive to the local NS office to pick up my food and get weighed in. This particular Saturday I had plans to go motorcycle riding with my friends after my appointment. I attended my appointment as usual, stepped on the scale, filled out my food order form, and while my food bag was being filled I had my one-on-one with my nutritionist. I grabbed my bag as I walked out the door, said goodbye to Jill at the desk, with whom I had become friends, and drove home.

Got home and emptied my bag to do my inventory and found that the NS folks had shortchanged me 3 freeze dried hamburgers. No problem…on a few occasions I found some things missing from my bag…hard to read my writing I guess. I called Jill and explained the situation to her; she suggested that I swing by the office on my motorcycle, pick up the burgers and just stuff them into my overnight bag…they were small enough that I could carry them with me for the weekend and drop them at my house afterwards…good plan, so I packed my overnight bag and left. Jill told me she would leave the burgers on the reception counter for me.

I got back to the NS office on my (admittedly) very loud Harley-Davidson Motorcycle. Dressed in my biker garb…black leather, black T-shirt, jeans, tattoos blazing…I walked into the office. I didn't recognize the woman behind the counter…must be new…but the burgers were there…I grabbed them, smiled at the woman, turned and walked out. Easy as you please…!

It should be noted here that only a few weeks earlier a local police officer had been gunned down in the area by a motorcycle gang member who was recently released from prison. Tensions (and suspicions) were high between the police and motorcycle riders. As I was driving home I noticed a marked police cruiser coming up fast behind me with its lights on…so instinctively I slowed down and pulled to the right. I coasted this way for a few hundred yards, waiting for the officer to pass me, but he never did…when I looked in my rearview mirror I noticed he was right on my tail, lights still flashing. I pulled over and waited for him to stop.

When he came to a complete stop I got off my bike so he could see both of my hands (a hint from my younger brother who was/is a police officer…ALWAYS make sure the police can see your hands…it puts them at ease). He immediately leaped from his car, gun drawn and pointed in my direction, yelling for me to stop moving…which I did immediately…! He gave me the standard instructions: on my knees facing him, hands behind the head, fingers interlaced, and lay face down on the shoulder of the road. He cuffed me, read me my rights, and removed my bag from my bike…without another word. When he tried to put me in his cruiser I protested: I never had the chance to remove the keys from my motorcycle, which was parked on the side of a busy street. He told me "You have bigger things to worry about buddy…" and said no more as I was shoved into the cruiser.

It was a quick ride back to the NS office. He walked me in…still cuffed…into the packed waiting room and up to the reception desk. He asked the girl at the desk "Is this the man?" and she nodded…he opened my bag and removed the three burgers and asked "Is this what he stole?" and she nodded. It wasn't until then that I understood what had happened: the new girl, not knowing me, thought I had stolen the burgers so she called the police. From her description of me and considering the tensions in the area at the time, an all points bulletin was put out on me. Since I was never asked to comment, and since I am smart enough to know that if you're a biker in that situation you NEVER speak until spoken to…I kept my mouth shut. He was just about to walk me out when Jill came out to the desk…she saw me…saw the cop…saw the scared look on the receptionist's face, and exclaimed "What in the hell is going on here?" It was then I finally got up the nerve to open my mouth, so I said "Hi Jill…apparently this girl thought I stole those burgers and this officer never asked me anything about it, so I THINK I was about to be booked for burger larceny…!" As a final parting blow to the dead-above-the-neck police officer, I asked "Is that a felony or a misdemeanor?"

Anyway, the rest of the story was sad…lost jobs, reprimands, apologies (LOTS of those, in person and in writing), and free food from NS for a month. Sometimes diet food can be more trouble than it's worth…!

Chapter 4: THE SECRET ANSWER TO WEIGHT LOSS: Finding _your_ formula…and some "tricks" that might help you succeed…!

"…I never promised you a rose garden…"

Lynn Anderson

"If being on a diet was easy it wouldn't start with the letters D-I-E…!"

Dr. Bill Dispoto

Here's what the weight loss industry seems afraid to tell you…not the diet gurus, the diet food manufacturers, the doctors, hospitals, nutritionists, therapists, or fitness experts: **the weight loss answer for YOU may not come from a single source**. YOUR solution…what I call YOUR FORMULA…may be a combination of SEVERAL sources of assistance. Some "parts" of your formula may be easy and some may be difficult…some may be popular and shared among many obese individuals while others may be personal just for you…some of them may be active and aggressive (such as diets or surgery) while others may be passive (such as meditation). The trick is to find the right "mix" for you…to find your FORMULA. If you're like me…and I cannot stress this enough…finding your formula may takes *YEARS* of trial and error. Think about that for a minute and let it sink in: YEARS of experimenting with different diet techniques before you find the right diet solution that suits you. While that possibility may seem discouraging at first, you MUST accept that weight loss is NOT an overnight effort. No magic genie is going to wave his/her magic wand and make the fat go away…once I accepted the fact that it took me YEARS to gain the weight I was able to accept the fact that the reverse process may take a similar amount of time…success is just as much a function of patience as it is perseverance and effort…!

Everyone who has ever been successful losing weight has a "trick" or "secret" that helped them in their effort. In fact, there is probably one trick for every person who has ever tried to lose a few pounds. Diets and surgery sometimes aren't enough…you have to augment the "active" effort with one or more "passive" tricks. Here are a few suggestions you might want to think about, plus a synopsis of what is working for me:

First, let's assume that you are NOT considering surgery as an option. That's good for me since I am certainly not in a position to recommend what type of surgery (see previous chapter) is best for anyone…for that information see you primary care physician who will refer you to a licensed bariatric surgeon. That having been established, **let's start with the active part of YOUR solution: finding the right diet for you**.

I have said this before but let me repeat myself for safety's sake: **never embark on ANY diet without first consulting with your primary care physician!** They know the physiological "you" better than anyone…they know what you are sensitive to, allergic to, and what ailments you have that will cause restrictions in your diet (low fat, low sodium, etc.). **Ask your PCP to recommend a licensed nutritionist as**

well…someone you can talk to, consult with…an expert who knows more about food and metabolic functions than you or your PCP. Once your PCP puts you on a diet, your nutritionist can recommend//approve the minor deviations/modifications to your diet so that you can find your "solution."

Your solution is the diet "formula" that works for you. You may find that the "by-the-book" Jenny Craig diet works well for you…by-the-book meaning that you follow Jenny's diet plan to the letter without ANY deviations. I recommend that you start here…with a by-the-book attempt at a diet that appeals to you. Maybe a modified Jenny Craig (or Nutrisystem or Lean Cuisine or any of the pre-packaged food diets…let's face it, they're all very similar) augmented with a restricted carb diet like Atkins if you are a carbohydrate addict like me.

What finally started working for me? A modified weight watchers plan that focuses more on number of servings than calories…I count portions of carbs (starches), meats (proteins), veggies, fruits, milk/dairy, and fats. All under a doctor's (and his in-house nutritionist) watchful eye, I am allowed (limited to) 8 servings of carbs and meats (the weight/measurement of each is about an ounce per serving), and 3 servings each of fruits, milk, and fat per day. Veggies are the inverse of the other food groups…instead of being limited to 3 servings per day, I am expected to eat AT LEAST 3 servings a day, but more is good as long as they are fibrous, non-starchy, and add vitamins or minerals to my diet. So whenever I can I load up on the leafy greens and vitamin powerhouses like cauliflower, broccoli, and carrots. I also incorporate packaged foods and even commercial foods into my diet whenever I can and within my diet's parameters. YES, that means that occasionally I may have a Nutrisystem main course with my noon meal or even a couple of slices from a Pizza Hut pizza. I still eat fast food (Popeye's fried chicken is at the top of my list, although I can't eat very much of it in one sitting…fat content you see..!) and Lean Cuisines and Medifast bars! I do this because I found that I needed more variety in my diet…my cooking skills are limited to mostly simple dishes and cooking for one is VERY hard when most recipes are intended for 6 to 8 servings. So I incorporate prepared foods once in a while to keep my diet interesting and palatable.

Hand in hand with the above suggestion is this tip: **get yourself a copy of the pamphlet entitled "Choose Your Foods: Exchange Lists for Weight Management"** by the American Diabetes Association (www.diabetes.org) and the American Dietetic Association (www.eatright.org). This book has become my bible…in it you will find crucial information about calories, servings, calories PER serving of each food group, and best of all, just like the title suggests…information about calories for many top selling commercial foods and meals from fast food establishments.

Another tip I have for you is to **wean the fat out of your diet slowly but steadily**. Yes, even the STRICTEST diet doctor will tell you that the human body needs SOME fat in its food intake to maintain its physiological processes, but unless you go on a strict vegan (NOT lacto-ovo vegetarian) diet there will ALWAYS be enough fat in the raw foods you use to prepare your foods (or, as in the case of using prepared foods like I do, EVERY packaged/commercially cooked food has sufficient fat in it) that you will not need to add more fat to your diet. Therefore, start looking at fat sources in your diet and start looking for low or no-fat substitutes for these foods. When I did this, I found that most of the processed fat in my diet came from these sources:

1. Eggs (cholesterol)

2. Half and half (in my morning coffee)

3. Butter/margarine/sour cream

4. Salad dressings (bleu cheese fan)

5. Cooking oil

So what I did was to find a substitute for these sources and begin replacing the fatty foods with their low/no fat counterparts. Cooking spray instead of cooking oil when frying, apple sauce as a substitute for oil when baking, egg white products instead of whole eggs, fat free cream cheese or FF sour cream or (the best and most healthy substitute) FF plain unflavored yogurt instead of butter/margarine/sour cream, and even fat free half n half in my coffee. My ½ and ½ was the hardest give-up…I LOVE my 1st cup of coffee in the morning, and the FF stuff just isn't the same, but I got used to it. The only category I was unable to substitute was fat-free salad dressings…so I simply limit the number of salads I eat on my diet. If you can imagine this: on my diet, a big salad with lots of crunchy greens and veggies, maybe some croutons, a little grated cheddar cheese, and a healthy dose of bleu cheese dressing is like my dessert…it's actually a TREAT instead of a TORTURE!

Next, **start READING LABELS and count servings or portions instead of calories**! Read and then use the bible…learn that all calories are NOT the same: i.e., fat calories are NOT the same as vegetable calories (you may be rolling your eyes right now but as smart as I am I had to learn that lesson the hard way!). Some calories stay with you longer than others due to their chemical composition. Once you learn what you should be eating and why…start looking for those types of foods when you go shopping…complex carbohydrates like veggies and fiber-heavy starches instead of the simple sugars like sucrose (processed or table sugar) and fructose (fruit sugar). Stay away from fat in the foods you buy…you can't eliminate it all together, but you CAN limit your fat intake by purchasing low-fat or fat-free (FF) alternatives when you shop.

Let me interject another tip here…one that I am SURE you have heard before: **never ever go shopping when you are hungry!** The old urban legend about the impulse buyer is a true one, at least in my case. I have gone on food shopping trips when I was hungry only to return home with bags full of food that I cannot eat…or at least foods that have so much fat, sugar, and cholesterol that they would take me MONTHS to eat them based on my exchange/serving allowances. What works best for me is a low-carb, high protein, high fiber energy bar and a big cup of coffee eaten just before I leave the house for the supermarket…it fills me up and rids me of that desperate feeling when I am shopping.

When you read the labels make sure that you "do the math"! Determine how many servings of each group are included in each "serving" of whatever you are buying (for example, the bible says that 15 grams of carbs = 1 serving of carbs). A "single portion" of a popular brand of canned chili has 2 servings of protein (the meat), 2 serving of carbs (the beans and sugar used in the prep process), and even 2 servings of fat...so when you eat 8 oz (single serving size) of that chili, you dip into at least 3 different nutritional groups (protein, carbs, fat) on your diet.

It's not a food group but it is something you want to track: **when shopping and cooking, watch the sodium!** The experts suggest that a normal non-dieting person should limit his/her sodium intake to no more than 2500 mg per day…and that aint much when you start reading how much salt is added in today's processed food.

This may seem silly and tedious, **but buy yourself a good food grade scale and start weighing your food**, at least in the beginning. Make sure it can read down to the tenth of an ounce and put it to use when you need it. Why do you need a scale when everything is seemingly already measured for you? Well, sometimes if you buy a "can" of something it may contain 2 servings of something…if the can contains 15 ounces of food, how are you going to know how much 7.5 ounces is without a scale? Here's another good example of when a scale might come in handy: the ADA bible gives a serving of cooked pasta (15 grams of carbs) as 1/3 of a cup…but as anyone who has ever cooked pasta you know that a cup of cooked elbow macaroni is a LOT more pasta (by weight) than a cup of cooked rigatoni (do I REALLY need to go into the details about size?). Therefore, best to WEIGH a cup of cooked pasta such as spaghetti and then use that weight next time you use larger pasta such as rigatoni or shells…just a suggestion!

Something else that helped me a lot…probably the single MOST helpful and productive exercise in my diet regimen and something you may want to consider doing on a daily basis: in addition to reading labels and weighing your food, **start writing your food intake down and keep a detailed diary of what you are eating, and BE HONEST**! Most bariatric doctors require this exercise as part of a pre-operation weight loss plan…yes, most if not all bariatric surgeons use a pre-op diet as an indicator to determine whether you are ready to adopt the new reduced calorie lifestyle. The intent is this: if you can't diet and lose weight before your surgery, the chances are slim that your surgery will be a long-term success. Part of my pre-op diet plan was to write down every serving of each nutritional group that I consumed during the day…kind of like a modified Richard Simmons Deal-a-Meal (for those of you who have tried Mr. Simmons' weight loss plan as I have). I was given 8 servings of protein, ditto carbs, and three servings each of low-fat dairy, fruits, fats, and at LEAST 3 servings of non-starchy veggies. I found that writing my consumption down kept me honest (a problem that I had in the past…lying to myself about how much food I ate during the day). With my trusty scale to weigh exact portions and my diary to track how many of my allowable portions I consumed, I found the order of it all…the regimen if you want to call it that…soothing and reassuring. My dad thinks that quirk was a product of my time in the military…when EVERYTHING in my life was planned and scheduled and orderly…every day was scripted like an itinerary. I really got into that lifestyle, and by imposing that same kind of order on my diet I found that I was able to stick to it better.

Now a few tips on **getting outside help**. As much as I pride myself on being disciplined enough to manage my diet by myself, I must admit that having help, no matter how insignificant or distant, is a good thing. The first suggestion I have is to **recruit a reliable and understanding diet buddy**. This is an endorsed characteristic of many successful diets like Weight Watchers. Find someone who is in your corner and can understand what you are going through. **A diet buddy, as I define it, is a person who you can discuss anything with related to your diet…food, eating, recipes, products, dieting options like fat camps and new pharmaceuticals, and even emotional feelings of shame (when you fall off the wagon?), pride (when you do something good), distress, impatience, and discouragement**. **A diet buddy is someone who you can call at 2 in the morning if you suddenly wake up with a craving for a half-gallon of Ben and Jerry's Ice Cream**…(have to give the movie "Fatso" starring Dom Deluise credit for that image: the 2 am phone call scene I just described was taken directly from that movie)! Clearly this means that the BEST diet buddies are friends who are dieting as well. Not all of us have friends who are obese (for example…me! As I said earlier in this book, not one of my childhood friends has gained so much as a pound since high school…!), so if you have to make a choice, pick someone who is dieting but may not necessarily be a close friend. **This is MY OPINION mind you, but I would rather have someone who truly understands my struggle** than someone who doesn't, no matter how close I may be with the latter. When I was working I had a workplace friend who was a great listener and was willing to tolerate hours of hearing me lament about how hard it was to stick to a diet…but this guy was stick thin, so he had really NO idea what it meant to be obese. As appreciative as I was for his patience and willingness to help me out, you get more empathy from someone who shares your plight.

You may also want to consider therapy and/or group meetings. When I was in the early version of Nutrisystem (both times I attended privately, no affiliation with any medical or professional organization) and Medifast (affiliated with Johns Hopkins Hospital when I attended) group therapy sessions were a main function of the system. I had personal sessions with nutritionists and group sessions with psychological therapists leading a group of obese patients in the same program. At first I hated and even resented these sessions, but after a time **I came to enjoy my personal and group therapy: I think my enjoyment stemmed from the old "misery loves company" syndrome. I found that my agony was less painful knowing that there were many people suffering just as much as me, and some even more! I found that comforting…not to mention the fact that I forged some solid friendships with the people in my groups**. Another advantage of meeting people this way is the group sessions are an endless source of "diet buddies" as discussed above: once you meet someone with whom you are comfortable sharing your intimate diet confessions with, use him/her as a diet buddy and offer him/her the same courtesy. You might find an invaluable source of support and comfort there!

Even though you may not want to use any of them as your emergency diet buddy, don't overlook the support, encouragement, and feedback of your family and friends: they can be an infinite source of assistance. My family, to whom this book is dedicated, was the rock and inspiration in my struggle. Some of the people closest to me were encouraging and supportive while others were (to my dismay) oddly harsh and suspicious, but I found that the mixture of approaches used by my family and friends to be therapeutic. One cannot exist on words of praise and encouragement alone: that is a formula for apathy and laziness and possible failure. One needs the occasional kick in the ass to stay sharp, focused, and honest…so make sure you seek the help, feedback, and judgment of someone who will provide you with that kick once in a while.

Beware the scale! The dieter's arch enemy, everyone knows that stepping on a scale is one of the least enjoyable tasks of a regular diet regimen…so you can't avoid them altogether. However, step on the scales wisely and regularly but not over-frequently. **The shortest frequency of scale readings is no more than once a month**: your body is going through a myriad of changes and your body weight can fluctuate several pounds depending on variants such as water retention, outside temperature, and the evil phenomenon we know as "plateauing." The LAST thing you need is the discouragement of stepping on the scale after two grueling weeks of dieting only to find out that you haven't lost ANY weight because unbeknownst to you your body is retaining water due to a cold spell! **Stepping on a scale once a month is MORE than enough to get an accurate snapshot of how your body is responding to your diet**.

Here is a personal tip from me to you: **find your incentive(s)…your motivation(s)…your reason(s) for wanting to be thin, and remind yourself of it (them) constantly…morning, noon, and night.** Here are a few favorite responses from some of my obese friends:

1. Maybe you want to be healthy enough again to play with your kids…this was the overall most popular choice among my married friends with children…and every one of them who described this incentive shed a tear as they did…clearly a very important consideration for parents!

2. Maybe you want to be able to enjoy more activities with your family like vacations that require physical exertion…ever tried to enjoy a day walking around Disneyland while carrying around an extra 50 lbs?

3. Maybe you want to get ahead in the office…or maybe, like me, you don't even HAVE an office but you want one. You're unemployed and you know that NO ONE will hire you looking as you do.

4. Maybe you want to get back outside and enjoy some physical activities or recreation…from simply taking a walk in the woods (one of my personal favorite activities that I haven't been able to enjoy for about 8 years now) to swimming, hiking, bungee jumping, ANYTHING that you can't enjoy anymore because of your weight.

5. Sex…need I say more? Physical attraction and interaction diminishes proportionately with weight gain…the fatter you get, the LESS you will get!

Once you shortlist your incentives, find ways to remind yourself about them…if that means painfully watching old home movies of your kids playing in the back yard while you sat in the lawn chair unable to participate…then watch them.

Most of us who diet know what "binging triggers" are: the stimuli that cause us to eat or overeat when we know we shouldn't. Some of us eat when we are under pressure; some of us eat when we are bored; and some of us like to eat while we are driving our cars. Did you know that there are triggers within your subconscious that can also help you to AVOID eating? I call them "strengthening triggers." **In line with that idea, the last thing I will suggest is that you look for YOUR strengthening triggers: those things…music, sounds, smells, poetry, maybe even faces, that remind you of what NOT being overweight is like and incorporate them into your daily lifestyle**. I call them strengthening triggers because they strengthen your will power and self control during those times when temptation seems overwhelming. My strengthening trigger…as silly as it sounds…is music from the 1970's. It reminds me of a happier, more peaceful, and less stressful time in my life when all I had to worry about was schoolwork, sports, my summer job(s), and keeping my bike (and once I began to drive, my dad's car) running so I could get around. More importantly, I was THINNER back then, so when I hear 70's music I am reminded of how happy I was back then…how happy I was when I was thin. When I get tense or I feel myself reaching for food when I know I shouldn't I simply turn on a 70's radio station (Bless my cable provider for running a 70's station 24 hrs a day!) and my mind creates that image for me…a younger, happier, THINNER version of myself. I find that image and nostalgic feeling sufficient motivation to avoid eating: 70's music reminds me of what it was like to be thin and the memory kick starts my desire to get back to that body image…and that's how it works for me.

Find a similar trigger for yourself: what helps you form the image of yourself as a thinner version of you? Whatever it is, keep it around…whether it's a photo, a song on your iPod, a poem, a story, or scripture from the Bible.

Well, that's the solution formula according to this author. If you are saying that my solution seems too simple, you're wrong. It took me years of dieting (see earlier chapters for just SOME of the diets I have tried) to find the right mix for me:

- The right diet and nutritional balance

- The right mixture of support sources…family, friends, specialists, and group therapy

- The right lifestyle changes…when to shop, what to look for, when/how often to weigh myself, tracking what I eat, etc.

It may take you some time, but once you find the right mixture for yourself I am confident that you will start to see positive results like I did! Good luck!

Chapter 5: Our culture isn't helping…it's a conspiracy I tell ya…!

So once again let me repeat: I am not blaming anyone for my condition! I did the eating, and I will take the blame for it. Having said that, here are a few organizations that contributed to my demise…!

Television is a prime culprit…but the real guilty ones are the companies that advertise on TV. Has anyone else noticed (or is this just an obese guy's obsession?) that it seems like every other commercial on TV is about a food product or at least features food prominently in the advertisement? Except for the election season when 3 out of 5 commercials are political hate-ads, almost 40% of all advertisements on TV involve food in some way, and that percentage goes up during the following times:

1. During the holidays

2. On the weekends during indoor sports seasons like football, hockey, and basketball

3. At nights during prime time

How is ANYONE, fat or normal-sized alike, supposed to maintain healthy eating habits when our senses are being constantly bombarded by a nonstop campaign of enticements like this? Fat people have a particularly hard time resisting these temptations; the main reason is our central preoccupation with food. In my introduction I suggested that food is like a drug to us…and we are the addicts. Imagine if you were a drug addict hooked on cocaine and on TV every day, every 10 minutes or so, were advertisements which showed people using cocaine…there they are, using coke at the dinner table, having it delivered in huge bags to the door, snorting a few lines with your coffee or orange juice before running out to work or school in the morning, and of course let's not forget those hilarious cocaine adds during the Super Bowl…! Sounds ridiculous right, an exaggeration? I'm blowing it out of proportion? Not really, because for a FOOD ADDICT like me that's what I go through every day...!! What's worse, I am a SHUT IN…I am a disabled Veteran collecting a disability pension, and my disability has forced me to be largely (no pun intended) housebound. So when I am not writing I am watching TV…there is NOTHING else for me to do…! So for 23 and a half hours every day, while I sit here in my house trying to eat healthy and lose weight, I am inundated with advertisements trying to get me to jump off the wagon…!

There is really no way for an obese person to describe the physiological or psychological assault they are forced to endure during these food commercials. For me it's like a trigger: every time a food ad comes on TV, it triggers a memory for me. My senses are heightened…I become like a fat Spiderman…! The MOST acute of my senses is my sense of smell…I can actually "smell" what is being advertised. Don't laugh…there is actual scientific research proving that our brains can retain olfactory memories for years, even if the experience (the smell) occurred only once in our lives. Have you ever seen a cinnamon bun commercial on TV and you SWEAR that you are standing in a Cinnabon store at the mall? You can actually SMELL the fresh hot buns cooking! The more "special" the memory is the more likely we are to retain it, and what's more special to a fat person than his/her relationship with food?

Then there is my sense of taste: I can actually "taste" the food I see commercials for, especially when I am VERY hungry. On my current diet I am trying very hard not to eat anything after 4 pm every day…ask any expert and they will say that a dieter should never eat anything close to bedtime. It has been explained to me by nutritionists that any food that is in your system when you are at rest has a better chance of being converted to fat…so I simply stop eating early in the day. Unfortunately late afternoon and evening is one of the most popular times for food ads. So when I am hungry, and I see a KFC commercial hawking a promotion for "12 pieces of Original Recipe and 3 large sides for $20", I can actually TASTE the chicken…that exquisitely greasy-salty secret combination of herbs and spices…!. Hell, even my sense of TOUCH gets involved here…because if I close my eyes I can almost FEEL the greasiness of the chicken in my hands!! The commercial provides the auditory and visual stimuli…the seeing and the hearing…and my addicted-yet-deprived system provides the rest…I can smell, taste, and feel the food (my fix) through my TV…! Sometimes it takes every bit of will power and self control that I can muster NOT to rush out of the house to "score."

Food ads, among other factors that I will discuss later, are contributing to my downfall, and there are a LOT of guilty parties. Take the prepared food industry for example...let's beat up on the fast food industry first. We all know that fast food is bad for us…even when taken in moderation most fast food products are high in fat, sodium, sugar, or additives. We've known this for years, yet little to nothing has been done. Oh sure, the fast food companies have added a few menu items that are supposed to be "healthy", but studies have been done that many of the salads, grilled sandwiches, and lean meats still contain unhealthy amounts of fat and sodium. And EVERYONE is guilty, without exception.

No, the trend is NOT towards the healthy but towards the volume, the size, and the weight. When was the last time any of you saw the major fast food companies competing on TV with their varieties of salads? No, what you see is them competing with their variation(s) on slow death. Take burgers for example: in the summer of 2010, Wendy's, McDonalds, and Burger King all came out with their version of the mega-burger. Their commercials were bent on out doing the other guy on size, "fixins", and variations (Burger King and McDonalds each came out with no less than 3 variations of their 1/3 pound burgers). Then there was the price war: since everyone basically had the same size burger, the only way to outdo the other guy was to reduce the price on their version.

And what about those burgers? Were they prepared with your health in mind? Of course they weren't…1/3 pound of ground beef is enough for an entire day's worth of protein. That alone should tell you that their concern was NOT for your health but for your desire for excess…and we all have it. OK…then maybe we can give them credit for the way the burgers were prepared? Burger King claims to "grill" their burgers, but time after time I have seen studies that suggest that the King's preparation method adds little to the overall healthiness of the final product.

OK…so they are all equally as guilty in their preparation method and the size of the burger…but how is it presented? What comes on the burger? Well, depending on whose burger you consider, additions include: massive amounts of processed cheese; sautéed or fried mushrooms and/or onions; sodium rich sauces like A1 Steak Sauce or BBQ sauce; and of course the ever present capillary-clogging king of them all…bacon…! Look at Wendy's entry in the Battle of the Burgers, "The Baconator." The 2010 version comes in three sizes: ¼ pound, ½ pound, and ¾ pound. Let's focus on the ¾ pound Baconator for a moment: that's THREE ¼ pound fried beef patties, each topped with cheese and three slices of bacon…not to mention all the standard fixins you could want. Should we give Wendy's credit just because they all come with the optional slice of tomato, onion, and a leaf of lettuce…nah, I didn't think so either. So do the math: 12 ounces (precooked…I have to say that or I could get sued) of beef, maybe 5 or 6 ounces of cheese, and approximately 6 to 8 ounces of bacon…all on ONE BURGER…!! I checked all of the diet literature I received when I went in for my bariatric surgery last year and do you know what it said? Just one ¾ pound Baconator contains enough meat for a single person for almost 2 days, enough dairy for 3 days, more sodium than a person should consume in a week and as much fat as the normal person should consume in a week and a half…!! So I ask for the first time of what will be MANY times in this chapter…is it any wonder we are all getting fat?

BUT, you're probably saying, what about those OTHER fast food franchises, the ones that don't serve burgers? What about Taco Bell, or KFC…what about Subway, where Jared got so skinny…aren't they looking out for our best interests? OK, let's look at what the OTHER franchises are offering as alternatives…to compete with the Burger Boys…well, there's KFC's "Double Down". You've heard of that one haven't you? Sure you have…here's what it's got on it: 2 fried Original Recipe chicken breast patties, 2 slices of cheese, and 2 slices of bacon (damn, that bacon is a popular condiment, aint it?). That's enough sodium for 2 weeks, fat for a week, and not a single redeeming quality. For all intents and purposes, it takes everything that's bad about KFC and rolls it up into one single product.

Subway had potential…I have to give them that. For a while they were advertising their light fare menu…the 6 and 12 inch veggie subs…tuna, light turkey and ham…but they have strayed from that path lately. Lots of celebrities in their commercials, but good, 'ole dieting Jared is not to be seen, at least not prominently anymore. Now the emphasis is all about their 5 dollar foot longs…with the meatball and Italian varieties front and center. GREAT alternative Subway…MORE FOOD at a LOWER PRICE…! So that's the next topic…fast food hawking low prices for more food.

When the recession started to hit, everyone in the fast food industry scrambled. No longer could mom and dad afford to feed their kids dinner from a fast food chain…not when Whoppers and Big Macs went for 3 to 4 dollars each. So how did the industry react to demand? The dollar menu of course…! Within a few months of each other, McDonalds was first I believe, almost every fast food chain created a dollar menu…or some variation of such. And the menus were complete too…each had its own sandwiches, side dishes, even desserts…some even had milk shakes and soft drinks…! The items on these menus were largely priced at $1.00 each, while some franchises decided to expand the menu with more items and developed a sliding price scale. Taco Bell for example has a discount menu with several dozen items on it…a much wider variety than the burger boys…with prices ranging from 89 cents to around $1.49. McDonalds has a value menu, and so does Burger King, Wendy's, Arby's, Sonic, and Dairy Queen.

Even upscale franchises like Boston Market are getting into the game…every summer (for the past 2 years at least) they have offered their "buy a family meal and get a 2nd chicken for 2 dollars" special. McDonalds and Burger King answered by lowering the price of their original burgers, their staples the Big Mac and the Whopper…they regularly run specials during which you can get these big burgers at special low prices if you buy them in quantity…such as BKs offer of 2 Whoppers for $4.

Pizza you say? They are no better…look at the recent pizza wars on TV advertising. First Dominos ran their "2 mediums with toppings for around $5 each" and then Pizza Hut jumped in the pool. They began running multiple specials that changed every so often…1st it was any large with up to 3 toppings for $10, but then rival Papa Johns chimed in and offered unlimited toppings on their large pizzas for $10…so Pizza Hut had to answer with a similar special of their own: their "any, any, any" special. Any crust, any size, any toppings for $10. When the offer gets old and stale, they simply repackage it under a different name or assumed title…like an NFL game day special…any large for $10, choose any toppings.

Another thing: can fast food chains make getting food any easier? The drive through service window is a big part of my downfall. They made getting food so easy that all a person has to do is get in the car and drive to the restaurant…no getting out of the car…hell, you don't even have to get dressed all the way to get fast food anymore (though I would not recommend that). And if you thought that by patronizing some of the fancier theme restaurants you could avoid the pitfall of the drive thru, no such luck. First there was Applebees "carside to go" service; you call your order in and they bring the food out to you in the parking lot. No moving, no getting out of the car, no social interaction required. A few other chains have implemented similar programs in order to compete with the fast food chains and each other…much to the downfall of the obese population.

So as a fat person…why am I complaining? Because we are going in the wrong direction: we are getting fatter as a society, so we should be decreasing the amount of food we are eating, but the fast food chains are increasing it…and they are making food easier to get for less money. Why is it that for around $10 I can get a regular salad at a place like Saladworks (one of my recent FAVORITE places to eat…I just wish it was serve yourself) and for the same money you can get enough food from the McDonalds or BK value menus to feed three people? McDonalds has their "McDouble"…a 99 cent double cheeseburger…and a dollar small fries, dollar apple pies (you get TWO for a dollar), and dollar small soft drinks. Three people can each get a burger, a small fries and a small soda (and fight over 2 apple pies) for the same $10 that I spend for one salad…that's lettuce, some cheese, croutons, and dressing. That bothers the logical part of my brain, the part that believes in equal food for equal cost…! So I have begun to rationalize to myself that if I eat something that costs the same as something else, I am basically getting the same amount of calories in each meal. For example: a $4 Lean Cuisine dinner has the same calories as a $4 value meal at Arbys…say 2 junior ham and cheese sandwiches and a small milk shake…! That sounds reasonable doesn't it? Of course it doesn't, but it highlights my next point, which is WHY DOES DIET FOOD COST SO DAMN MUCH?

My local Italian restaurant and pizzeria sells (and delivers) a GREAT Chicken Parmesan dinner for around $10…it has a LARGE serving of chicken (it is so big maybe it's more accurate if I call it an UNHEALTHY portion of chicken), a LOT of spaghetti, an Italian roll with butter, and a small dinner salad. Then we have your typical diet chicken parmesan dinner…cost about $4…Lean Cuisine, maybe Weight Watchers, any of the commercial favorites…you get a piece of chicken that is about the size of a half-dollar and a side of pasta that would not satisfy an infant. I weighed the dinner from the restaurant and it came to about 32 ounces…that's 2 pounds of food not including the roll and salad. The diet meal weighed less than 8 ounces…so let's do the math:

32 ounces of food delivered and prepared by a restaurant for $10

8 ounces of food frozen and prepackaged sold in a supermarket for $4

In the same approach as my local Italian place, places like Chili's, Outback Steakhouse, and Applebee's, theme restaurants that can't exactly compete with the burger FF chains because of their primarily sit-down environment and higher prices, are offering 2 for 1 specials…where a customer can order a single appetizer and two entrees for prices like $20 or $25. I know there are a lot of people out there who are probably criticizing me for complaining about these kinds of pricing techniques, but from the perspective of a dieter it makes losing weight very difficult when the "bad food" is priced so much less than the "good" food. The results are obvious: you can get 4 times the food (32 ozs vs. 8 ozs in the case of my Italian restaurant) for only about twice the money from the restaurant…and the food is fresher, served hot, better tasting, but admittedly probably higher in calories and sodium than the frozen dinner. Is it any wonder, in these tough economic times, why fat people have no incentive to diet when they KNOW they are being cheated by the diet industry? But more on that later…

Since we introduced the subject, let's talk about supermarkets for a moment. Are they the alternative to fast food and restaurants? Are they the salvation I need as a fat person? Well, maybe they are and maybe they aren't. If I have to drive to the supermarket, get out (in public), walk the store…then maybe that would be my incentive to buy things that are good for me and avoid buying the wrong things. In my chapter about going out and interacting with the public there is a lengthy discussion about how uncomfortable it is for a morbidly obese person to go out in public…and just knowing that "the eyes" are on you, watching what you buy…may be enough to scare an obese person straight. The problem with the 21st century is that you don't even have to leave your house…EVER…if you play your cards right and know where to go online for your needs. So many supermarkets now have delivery services from their websites…every product on their shelves are listed on their website and for only a small premium and maybe a small delivery charge you can have your groceries delivered right to your door…and with that, there goes the incentive to buy smart and lean…my local delivery service recently shut down and none too soon for me…I was in the habit of buying every other week and my orders were full of fatty main courses and entrees, sweet baked goods like pies and cakes from the store's bakery, snack cakes and donuts, and starchy side dishes like French fries and potato skins.

Why not just buy the prepared diet foods then? Forget that you are paying THREE TIMES more for each pitifully small serving of frozen food than it's really worth…suck it up, admit (and accept) the injustice, and drive on…! Well, that strategy sounds reasonable except for the fact that the selection among the commercial diet brands is VERY limited. "WHAT…?!" you say "…there are several brands of frozen diet foods, and each brand has a good quantity of meals to choose from." That may be true, but consider this: every brand has a variation on the most popular meals, and when you factor these out, the variety overall is not so broad. In other words, Healthy Choice, Lean Cuisine, Weight Watchers, and Smart Ones ALL have their variation on classics like chicken parmesan, meatloaf and potatoes, and turkey and stuffing. Assuming for a minute that there isn't much anyone can do with roast turkey or chicken parmesan to distinguish one variety from another, are we REALLY talking about 12 choices here (4 companies x 3 dinners) or only 3? I have tried these meals from each of these manufacturers and while all are good, they all taste basically the same…the only differences seem to be in weight and portion size. Other diet meals are not available everywhere, such as Michelina's and Trader Joe's…some of the meals produced by these manufacturers received high praise in WebMD's article entitled "The Best Frozen Dinners" written by Kathleen M. Zelman (http://www.webmd.com/food-recipes/features/best-frozen-dinners), but when I tried to find them in my local supermarket I had no luck. For any diet to be successful, most experts agree that you need texture, taste, and selection…without these three important qualities, eating diet food over the long haul is boring and bland and a dieter will lose interest quickly.

There are some services out there that will deliver fresh–made food right to your door on a daily basis…doesn't that sound perfect??!! Considering all of the complaining I have been doing about my dieting limitations, whether perceived or real, a daily delivery service appears to be the answer for me. No ordering from fast food restaurants…no ordering too much food from restaurants that deliver…no shopping in supermarkets with all of the enticements they have…no trying to cook for myself and serving myself 3 times as much food as I should be eating. Nope, just 3 tasty, fresh-cooked, filling meals delivered to my door every day…hell, even if I cheat I can only cheat with a day's worth of food…no more eating five Healthy Choice dinners in one sitting just because "…they were there." Services like "The Fresh Diet", which now delivers in Philadelphia,(www.thefreshdiet.com) offers meals delivered daily and meal packages for 7, 14, 21, or 30 days at a time. The more meals you order at a time, the less it costs…UH-OH…did I just mention COST??!! Yup, you guessed it: at the time of this printing Fresh Diet's premium service costs $420/week ($60 a day, for three meals and two snacks) or $1395/month (about $47 a day) if you order a month at a time…that's more than my mortgage payment…for DIET FOOD…!! Of course I understand that there are costs involved such as preparation, handling, and transportation, but a person could eat cheaper if they ate in a restaurant three times a day. I did the math and discovered that my favorite meals for breakfast, lunch, and dinner at my favorite diner come to about $35 a day WITH GRATUITIES…so how is that fair?

What about those "all you can eat" and low-price specials you see increasing all over? I don't remember what comedian first used this line, but it has always stuck in my head: we are not SUPPOSED to eat all we can eat…!!

1. Red Robin restaurants, while not one of my PRIMARY burger targets, has been running (at the time I wrote this book) a lot of commercials endorsing their specialty burgers, I presume in response to the Big 3's mega-burger offerings of summer 2010. So here is Red Robin with its own ½ pound variety of a burger, but to make matters worse, they offer what they call the "bottomless steak fries." Their carbohydrate "side dish of choice" for all of their gourmet burgers is a thick cut French fry…clearly not the best choice nutritionally or calorically…and they allow you to eat ALL THE STEAK FRIES YOU WANT DURING A SIT-DOWN DINNER…! A sound marketing strategy…but are they friggin insane?

2. Theme restaurant giants such as Chili's and Applebee's have also gotten into the "endless" or "all you can eat" game too. Chili's "endless" lunch special, where lunch customers can order and eat all the soup, salad, and nacho chips/dip that they want. Applebee's all you can eat Riblets platter…where you can order all the boneless pork ribs you want. If there

is one food on earth that a human being should NOT eat all-they-can-eat it is pork ribs…full of fat and (if processed) sodium.

3. The Olive Garden and their "endless pasta bowl" and "unlimited soup, salad, and breadsticks" lunch…c'mon OG, give us a gastrointestinal break…! The endless pasta bowl allows you to choose any pasta (from a menu of seven individual types of pasta) and any sauce (from six sauces) and you can keep ordering pasta and sauce until you choke on it…changing each time you order or ordering the same thing over, and over, and over again. The "unlimited…" lunch is not as bad since it includes soup (not TOO bad for you) and salad (actually good for you if you watch the fatty dressing), but still…do we NEED all we can eat?

4. The Golden Corral is a good place to eat…true, it may never get 4 or 5 stars in the AAA traveler's handbook, but the food is good, hot, and reasonable. The only problem, again, is the quantity…! GC is a buffet style restaurant, meaning you can eat as much of EVERYTHING as you can stuff into your face…the "special" changes frequently…sometimes it's a steak bar, sometimes seafood, sometimes Mexican…but there is always a salad bar, dessert bar, veggie bar, and entrée bar, all of which are "all you can eat." Other restaurants of this ilk include Old Country Buffet, HomeTown Buffet, Luby's, Ryan's Steakhouse, and the old Ponderosa

and Sizzler Steak houses. (I use the term "old" because every Ponderosa and Sizzler within driving distance of my home in New Jersey has closed over the past 15-20 years…which is good for me, since they were two of my FAVORITE places to go…!)

5. The pizza chains have entries in this category too, with popular chains Cici's, Chucky Cheese, Gatti's, and Shakey's pizza now serving an endless and all you can eat pizza and sometimes pasta buffet.

6. Even seafood has it's culprits; Red Lobster runs its yearly "endless shrimp" special, where you can choose from several varieties of shrimp cooked several ways, allowing the patron to eat as much of any kind (or multiple kinds) of shrimp they want. In the fast-food-seafood category, Long John Silver's (LJS) is offering its $10 family meal…multiple pieces of fried chicken, fried hush puppies, and side dishes (several of which are also fried). While this doesn't exactly fall into the all-you-can-eat category, it still fortifies the focus of the FF industry: more food for less money.

7. I saved these two for last because even though they have admittedly broken the cardinal rule against dieting, they offer a fare that is LARGELY health based. There are two "salad bar" buffet chains out there that offer an all you can eat experience that is aimed at the health

conscious: <u>Sweet Tomatoes and Souper Salad</u>. I have not patronized either of these establishments in a long time but from what I can remember each offers a generous salad bar, bread bar, and soup bar. If you choose to eat in, you may purchase the all you can eat special…but if you decide to take-out you can get one-time fill containers to take home with you…one container for your salad, one for your soup, and one for bread…at a good reasonable price. My research suggests that maybe both of these establishments also now offer a hot food bar similar to the hot finger-food bars presented by Sizzler and Ponderosa…with chicken wings, meats, veggies, potato and rice side dishes, and maybe even desserts, but I have not confirmed this…maybe I am afraid to, since confirming that suspicion will cause me to lose respect for them…! Right now, a salad bar is the ONLY place an overweight person should be eating "all they can eat"…!

Finally, has anyone else noticed how universally accessible food has become? Aside from the convenience of delivery services described above, do you realize that you can get ANYTHING from a fast-food burger to groceries to a fresh salad to a packaged taco dinner at ANY time of the day or night now? With all the entire food industry competing for your food dollar, and with competition getting fierce, we have become a 24-hr a day EATING society. When I was young restaurants and grocery stores had what were known as "business hours"; anyone in my age range will remember that quaint old tradition…! Stores would "open" in the morning and (I know this may seem hard to believe) would "close" in the evening. Most of them would be open on the weekends too, but their hours were "reduced"…that meant the proprietors would open for a shorter period of time on the weekend, giving their workers some time to spend with their families. I KNOW, FREAKY HUH?!

OK…I joke about it, but has the direction in which our society has gone really for the best? Do we REALLY need to buy groceries at 3 am? Here are just a few examples of what's out there…from a fat guy who has patronized EVERY one of them at one time or another:

1. Convenience stores are the primary culprits responsible for starting the 24-hr trend, providing round-the-clock access to things like candy, chips, sodas, and ice-cream…but if you wanted REAL food all that the convenience store offered were things like microwavable cheeseburgers and plastic-wrapped stale tuna or egg salad sandwiches…and only the MOST desperate of food junkies would partake of those gastric abominations. Nowadays, the mega-convenience store chains like WaWa's, Albertson's, and Sheetz offer fresh deli counters, fresh made salads, and fresh cooked sandwiches and hot dogs…and they are keeping these services open all night long…hey, doesn't everyone need and deserve a 1/3 pound hot dog at 3 in the morning? Isn't that one of our God-Given rights as Americans?

2. There have always been 24-hr diners and restaurants, especially in my home state of New Jersey, but now it seems that any restaurant that chooses NOT to stay open all night is doomed to fail…think about it…where would YOU go during daylight hours? Will you go to the place at the corner that's open at 6 am for breakfast…or maybe that cool all-nite place where you got that killer club sandwich that night after Joe's bachelor party? Iconic 24-hour a day places like Denny's and Waffle House are now getting competition from places like IHOP, The Cracker Barrel, and Perkins Family Restaurants.

3. Grocery store chains all have 24-hour franchises now…some of them sell only what was left on the shelves from the day shift, but more and more of them are keeping the salad bar, the hot food, the bakery, the deli, the produce section, and the fresh meat/seafood departments open all night long as well.

4. Fast food restaurants are quickly becoming places where you can "eat anytime of the day or night." Taco Bell even had a marketing campaign calling their late-night menu an opportunity for a "Fourth Meal"…forget obese people like me, do ANY of us need a fourth meal of fatty, sodium-filled Mexican food at 3 am?

5. How about mega-giants like Wal-Mart? With one on every corner now, and most with prepared food sections or cafeterias Wal-Mart has become just one more convenient place where an obese person can get food at 3 in the morning.

6. Think the pizza chains are blameless? Think again…on September 17, 2010 Lisa Cornwell of The Huffington Post reported that Domino's had just opened their first 24 hour restaurant in the United States… in southwestern Ohio near the University of Dayton. Anybody want to guess how long it will be before Pizza Hut and Papa John's get into the act?

   http://www.huffingtonpost.com/2010/09/17/dominos-pizza-opens-first-us-24-hour-store_n_721802.html

7. Finally, even the donut giants are getting into the game. Dunkin Donuts and Krispy Kreme have started opening stores that stay open all night long. I have tried the products at some of these locations (thinking fondly back to my traveling days, when a bagel and cream cheese at 3 in the morning on my way back from a car trip to Florida felt like less of a sin than a sackful of $1 double cheeseburgers from McDonalds) and the quality leaves a lot to be desired…apparently being open 24 hours a day doesn't mean that what they sell will be MADE 24 hours a day…but who

can complain? If you want a 4 am dozen donuts, you gotta take what you can get…!

So NOW do you agree with me that it all seems like a conspiracy? Everyone from the fast food industry to the grocery industry to the restaurant business seems to be in on it…a non-stop bombardment of convenience, poor nutritional choices, and price-inflation…! If not, let's consider the MAIN culprit in the conspiracy…the guiltiest party of them all…the diet industry.

Obesity is a pandemic in this country, and we are getting fatter by the day…MORE of us are becoming obese and those of us who are already obese are becoming MORE obese. The country's reaction to this disease was NOT to fight it at the source (aka, prevention). We prefer instead to react to the disease' effects…just like our embrace of abortion as a cure for pregnancy rather than promoting the use of protection…just like our embrace of the chemical cocktail as a treatment for AIDS rather than promoting safe sex…just like our embrace of litigation and medical treatment as a means to address the deadly effects of smoking rather than consider the ban of tobacco products completely (oops, did I offend anyone there?)…we would rather treat the effect of the disease rather than consider the prevention of it. If you don't believe me, read back a few pages and tell me how our culture has approached this disease: have we made any great strides lately in the direction of getting society to eat healthier? Sure, there are concerned citizens like First Lady Michelle Obama who fight obesity first hand and they should be applauded for their efforts…but they are falling on deaf ears. The reason is clear: our economy stands to lose too much if "obesity" were to just "go away." Look at the facts:

The diet industry is made up of several multi-BILLION dollar subcultures that pump massive amounts of money into the economy. What do you think would happen to this country if the following sub-industries were to fail?

1. The exercise industry…including equipment manufacturers, gymnasiums, personal instructors, etc. Imagine if every gym closed due to lack of enrollment.

2. The diet food industry…including the frozen, commercially-available varieties discussed earlier and pre-packaged, vacuumed-sealed varieties like Medifast and NutriSystem, and supplements like protein powder, vitamins, and stimulants. Imagine if NO ONE ever needed these products again.

3. The literary industry…self help books, recipe books for the obese, motivational books, etc. Imagine if every book geared to the obese person was removed from the shelves.

4. The medical industry…within this sub-industry are several branches:

a. Nutritionists and those who specialize in creating caloric-control diets

b. There's the doctors who specialize in the treatment of obesity related conditions…heart, diabetic, vascular, and even chiropractic, to name just a few

c. There's the bariatric industry…doctors who specialize in surgery for the obese…gastric bypass, lap banding, roux en y

d. There's the cosmetic surgery industry…doctors who specialize in tummy tucks, liposuction, skin reductions

e. Finally, there's the pharmaceutical industry…that group of unscrupulous individuals who provide over priced medications for all of the medical professionals listed above

I don't want to sound like a conspiracy theorist, but it is beginning to smell like our culture doesn't WANT obesity to go away…a cure would topple a good slice of our economy. And when you look at the direction our culture is going, all evidence points to perpetuation rather than elimination of the problem.

Now a word on some specialty groups within the obese community…the 1st being the National Association to Advance Fat Acceptance (http://www.naafaonline.com/dev2/) aka NAAFA. I must admit to having mixed feelings about groups like NAAFA; on the one hand, they are committed to ridding society of discrimination against the obese, which is one of the main topics of this book, and in that respect I support and applaud them. On the other hand, however, they have sent representatives to shows such as Dr. Phil preaching a platform of "personal acceptance", the argument being that they have reached the conclusion that it's OK to accept yourself as fat. They claim that they have accepted themselves as fat; that they are happy and satisfied with their body image; and they are perfectly content being obese. Now, never let it be said that I would EVER try to impose my will or belief system on anyone else…live and let live I always say…so if the leaders (reps) of NAAFA want to accept themselves as obese…and if they are TRULY happy with themselves as they say they are (and I have my doubts about that, but I won't call them liars either), then I say "fine" and "let them be." The problem in my estimation is the message this kind of philosophy sends to our non-obese neighbors. I did some research (see the results in chapter 7) and one of the recurring stereotypes about overweight people is that we are failures: we have no pride in ourselves as human beings, we have no self control over our appetites, and we have given up in the struggle to lose weight and get healthy. Our non-obese neighbors see us as "inferior human beings" because of our condition! The philosophy that NAAFA preaches feeds this harmful stereotype and gives rise to the prejudice against us. Overeating is an addiction and obesity if a disease, just like drug addiction, smoking, and alcoholism. Would the members of NAAFA suggest to a smoker or a drug addict or an alcoholic that they give up the fight against their addiction and accept it…even EMBRACE it?! Of course they wouldn't…it would be the HEIGHT of foolishness to suggest that they give up on themselves or that we as a society give up on those who need help with their afflictions. So to my NAAFA friends, whose fight seems so noble on the surface I sadly must say that **I agree with our non-obese neighbors: that anyone who is unhappy with their physical form and still accepts themselves as obese has adopted a defeatist attitude…it's a cop out for someone who has surrendered to the struggle…a LOSER. Furthermore, any organization that endorses reaching such an irresponsible conclusion by anyone within their ranks, especially an organization that is supposed to be an advocate for those afflicted with obesity, should be ashamed of themselves…you are helping NO ONE with that philosophy!.**

Then we have the "antichrists" of the obese movement…what I like to call the "deviant fringe element." Dr. Oz called the fetish "feeder-ism" (http://www.doctoroz.com/episode/fattest-women-america-face-off?video=12095)…morbidly obese women (mostly) who "pornographically" cater to an audience of deviant men who like to watch them eat. They operate "pay-as-you-watch" websites where these women, some dressed in "minimalistic outfits", some in lingerie, and some allegedly naked, engorge themselves with food to the apparent delight of their male audiences. Once again, under normal circumstances I wouldn't criticize these women and what they do to earn money: the 1st Amendment and Freedom of Speech gives them the right to operate these sites, and in my opinion if the "act" is legal and it doesn't hurt anyone in its execution then I say let them have their fun…it is not my cup of tea, but to each his own. However, in this case these women ARE hurting someone: they are hurting the cause of obese people everywhere! These women go on shows like the aforementioned Dr. Oz seemingly for no other apparent reason but to publicize themselves to generate more customers. They claim that they "love themselves" just as they are…each one topping the scales at 300 lbs+. One of them, who shall remain nameless (I will NOT give her the satisfaction of more free publicity in this book!), is currently over 700 lbs and has stated that it is her goal to become the fattest human being ever. She has been profiled on several shows, most recently because she has allegedly gotten engaged; one of her Internet "clients" has asked her to marry him. Her latest appearance was a brief sound bite about her wedding dress: a dress that will require more than 5 times the "normal wedding dress" amount of material to make!

My issue with these deviants is simple: they are an embarrassment to obese people everywhere. The rest of us (obese people) fight hard against the stereotypes about obese people. It is the "inferior human being" stereotype again…we're seen as fat, lazy, stupid, shameless, ignorant animals. We ask our non-obese neighbors to accept us as we are…to NOT see us as inferior to anyone else…we ask them to treat us the same as anybody else because we ARE the same as anybody else. Then they watch shows like Dr. Phil and Dr. Oz and see these women making complete fools of not only themselves but of obese people everywhere, making us all seem gross, disgusting, and abnormal: just as we find ourselves taking a step forward against discrimination, prejudice, and bullying we are forced to take two steps back because of people like this.

I laugh sometimes when I talk to my fat friends about rumors about a "miracle pill" or a medical treatment that could cure obesity in one fell swoop…I compare it to other legends like the water-fueled vehicles, the flying car, or the perfect solar-powered engine…an urban myth that is out there but would cost so much in the form of the destruction of the nation's economy that we may NEVER see such a miracle…Ahhhh, if only I were a rich man (don't worry, I'm not going to break into my "Fiddler on the Roof" impression) I could hire someone to help me diet…because I am beginning to fear that the only way I am going to be successful dieting is if I hire a full-time dietician/nutritionist like Oprah has!

Chapter 6: The great "What is good for you and what is bad for you" debate

WARNING: This is the chapter with a lot of research, facts, and data…and the results of all that research is **a LOT of conflicting information on percentages, word definitions, interpretations, and opinions**…that conflict being the main focus of this chapter. Some of what I will reveal in this chapter is what I call "no shit" information…information that, when you hear it, something like "too much sugar is bad for you", you immediately say "no shit." What I'm hoping is that maybe you'll also learn a few new things too, so keep this book handy next time you are trying to figure out what to serve your family and how much of it…!!

For decades overweight people have relied on the medical profession, the food industry, and even our own federal government to tell us what is "good for us" and what is not. If you think about it, how would the average person know what to think and what to eat without the research done by the so-called "experts?" Before the great "what is good for you" debate started, for YEARS at breakfast we ate bacon, ham, and eggs by the pound, toast covered in butter, sugary preserves, jellies, and honey, sausage gravy made with 100% pure animal lard slathered generously over biscuits made with that same lard, and everything covered in melted cheese (well, maybe not the toast)…that is until the Food and Drug Administration (FDA), the United States Department of Agriculture (USDA), and the American Medical Association (AMA) told us that EVERYTHING we were eating for breakfast was bad for us…!!

So here we are after literally decades of research and one would assume that we have it figured out by now, right? We should know by now what is good for us, what is bad for us, how much of what we can (or should) eat and how often, and with labeling having become so popular recently, all of this information should be CLEARLY marked on the packages of the food we buy, that information provided in clear and easy-to-understand language…RIGHT??!!

Not a chance…! Despite all of the research and wrangling over weights, measures, and labeling definitions, most people today still admit with some shame (not their fault…!) that they really don't know how much fat (saturated or otherwise) they should get, how many carbohydrates and in what form (complex or simple) they should get, what sweeteners are OK and which are not, and on, and on, and on…!

Whose fault? It depends on who you ask…but it shouldn't be that way, since there are those we are supposed to trust who are appointed by our elected officials to make things clear for us…that is, until you realize as I did that every player in this food game has their own agenda…their own "plan" which may NOT include being totally forthcoming to us the consumers. In other words, it seems that SOME organizations…who are supposed to be working FOR us…APPEAR to be working for someone else!!

Let's start with eggs…one of my favorite pet peeves since in my 50 or so years on this plant I have heard eggs vilified as a nutritional demon and then inversely canonized and worshipped as a nutritional and dietary staple…and this flip-flop cycle occurs about every five years or so…just long enough a period of time to go from one research study to another…!! Of course you have the egg growers of America…no need to state their objective, since their agenda is clear: get people eating as many eggs as possible, regardless of the danger or damage to our health…!

Cholesterol comes from 2 places: the cholesterol that your body produces and that which you receive from eating. The "good cholesterol" is called high density lipoprotein or HDL and the bad cholesterol is called low density lipoprotein, or LDL. Most of the LDL in your system comes from the foods you eat, and I think we can all agree that "bad" cholesterol was given that name for a reason: if too much LDL circulates in the blood it will build up on the walls of arteries and can restrict the flow of blood to the brain, the heart, or other important organs. When mixed with other bad compounds it can also form plaque, a hard substance that will also restrict the flow of blood and make the arteries less flexible…if a clot forms it can result in a heart attack or stroke.

So we are all in agreement that cholesterol is a bad thing, and eggs contain large amounts of cholesterol…hence, if A = B and B = C, then A MUST = C; eggs in their unaltered form (not counting egg white products or reduced cholesterol products like "Egg Beaters") are good in some respects but <u>very bad</u> in others. How bad are eggs you ask? Well, **in 2012 a research group from Canada released a study that compared the cardiovascular danger of eating egg yolks to smoking cigarettes!** So here are the facts about the (borrowing the catch phrase from that old pro-egg commercial) "incredible, edible, egg"…1 extra large egg provides:

- A LOT of protein, which is great…almost 7 grams, which for a relatively sedentary (the politically correct word for "lazy") male adult, who should be getting about 70+/- grams of protein a day, one egg contains about 10% of your total recommended daily intake of protein.

- Only about 80 calories, which is also good…that means that a 4 egg omelet if cooked with a low-cal cooking spray, only has about 320 calories…unless you also consider that of those 80 calories, 50 of them are fat calories…which is equal to about 63% of the total 80 calories…so as much as I like eggs, that is just TOO much…!!

- Almost 10% (6g) of your DRV of fat, all of which is saturated fat…that's just ONE EGG folks!

- About 3% (78 mg) of your DRV of sodium

- Cholesterol is the deal-breaker, because depending on who you ask, a person's "daily recommended value" (DRV) of cholesterol differs greatly. A single extra-large egg contains about 240 mg of cholesterol, which is:

  - About 80% of your DRV of cholesterol if you are a non-dieter eating a 2000 cal per day diet or…

- About 120% of your DRV of cholesterol if you are dieting and trying to maintain an 1800 cal per day diet…**that means that you get MORE THAN one day's worth of cholesterol in one egg…!! In other words…if you are dieting, you should not be eating whole eggs at all!**

Speaking of fats, cholesterol being one, what about OTHER forms of fats? There are animal fats such as butter and lard…vegetable fats such as vegetable oils…and now even artificial fats like olean, aka Olestra. Those who are dieting should be concerned about fats every second of every day: fats are almost completely retained by the body in their original form. Like protein, fat is a naturally occurring compound in the human body, and since it is the most dense when it comes to calories (WAY more calories in a gram of fat than a gram of protein or carbohydrates) and hardest to break down, the body does not burn ANY new fat introduced into your system. That means that virtually EVERY excess calorie of fat you eat is stored in your system in its original form. OK, so we know that fats are bad for us (that's one of those "no shit" moments I warned you about), but which "fat" is LESS bad for me than all of the others?

We all know that entire BOOKS have been written about the dangers of fats…who hasn't heard about the evils of trans fats, tropical oils, and saturated fats? I won't go into lengthy detail about the what's and why's here, because that's not what this book is about…but here is a quick synopsis condensed from several websites that talk about the dangers of fats:

- Saturated fats and trans fats are the bad ones…these are products or by-products from animal sources (butter is high in saturated fat because it is a product of cow's milk; similarly, cooking lard is high in both saturated fat and trans fat because it is simply rendered animal fat that has been processed for long term storage). Stay away from these as much as you can…and if you can cut these from your diet completely, you will do yourself a favor. Everyone agrees with this advice, from doctors to nutritionists to the friendly folks who raise animals for the meat you find in the market!

- Monounsaturated (monos) and polyunsaturated (polys) fats are the "not so bad" ones…mainly (but not solely) from plant sources. These fats can even be good for you in some ways…monos for example can improve blood cholesterol levels and benefit blood sugar levels, a bonus for those with type 2 diabetes. However, don't get too excited…**they contain just as many calories per gram as their saturated and trans cousins**…but if you have to include fats in your diet, you should make them monos or polys.

- So if the food industry can make artificial sweeteners (THAT discussion is coming up next) in so many forms, why can't they make an artificial fat-product that acts like regular fat but has none of the adverse "weight-gaining-artery-clogging" side effects of regular fat? Well, they did…or at least they TRIED: enter the product named Olean…aka Olestra…a fat substitute that adds no calories or fat to your cooking. Sounds great, but what is it? Olestra is a food additive submitted by Proctor and Gamble for approval to the FDA in 1996. Initially the only *intended* use for Olestra was in the manufacture of potato chips and early sales showed a great deal of success…that is, until the alleged adverse side effects of the compound became known. Olestra is rumored to cause a condition known as "steatorrhea"…a slightly less prolific condition closely related to diarrhea. Olestra causes abdominal cramping, loose (and in some cases uncontrollably loose) stools and anal leakage. Due to the side effects of the compound and news of said effects spreading through the consumer base, P&G suspended their plan to widen the use of Olestra in other applications such as cooking oils, margarines and salad dressings. I guess if you are a person who simply HAS TO HAVE fat-containing products you have to decide which is worse: eating regular fat and gaining weight or eating fat-substitutes and running the risk of (pardon my vulgarity here) shitting yourself. Hey, there are always adult diapers, right?

Well, there you have it…fats in a nutshell (no pun intended…and no knock on the nut industry!). Like eggs, fats are a nutritional group better cut from your diet…completely if possible, but at least as much as you can stand.

What's next? Well, we hinted at it earlier in this chapter, but how about the great "sweetener" debate, which includes topics such as:

Sugar: is it good or bad? If it's "OK in moderation" like the commercials tell us it is, should it be processed cane sugar (white table sugar) or sugar in the raw (brown sugar…unprocessed and retaining some of its natural molasses)? Where do "other" natural sweeteners such as honey come into the picture? How about fruit sugar commonly known as "fructose"…if it's naturally occurring in fruits, and we know that fruits are good for us…why can't we have as much fructose as we want?

The bottom line is that sugar, in all of its processed or unprocessed forms, is a carbohydrate (let's call them carbs shall we?) with little, if any, nutritional value. It is the basic and most common source of fuel for your body…which is good…unless you ingest too much of it. ANYTHING that the body gets too much of can be converted to FAT storage…that is part of our evolutionary heritage…something that scientists (anthropologists?) have suggested developed when we were cavepeople and food was scarce. Our bodies learned to adapt to periods of decreased food intake by storing up excess food in fat cells when it was plentiful. Without trying to get too "technical", our bodies are composed of basically three elements: water (~70%), protein (muscles, skin, organs), and fat. Whatever we put into our bodies has to be converted or broken down into one or more of these elements before it can be used or stored by the body. Therefore, excess fat, carbs (sugars, starches), and proteins (meats, dairy, legumes) are stored in the body as fat. Carbs act as the fuel for our cell functions while proteins are used to build up or replace the structure of our muscles and organs. If you ingest (eat) just the right amount of carbs, fat, and proteins…that means, the EXACT AMOUNT of energy calories your cells need to fuel the body and an equally EXACT AMOUNT of protein to maintain your body's structure…then you will maintain an ideal weight. If however you eat too much…you will gain weight. I read somewhere that for every 10 EXTRA calories of carbs you put into your body, 8 of those calories are turned into fat and the other 2 are burned during the conversion process (turning carbs into fat). On the other hand, for every 10 extra calories of protein you eat, 2 calories make it to your fat cells and 8 are burned up in the conversion process. The difference lies with the chemical make-up of the molecules themselves…*a carb molecule is easily broken down and converted, so the body doesn't need to burn too much energy converting it to fat*…not so with a protein molecule.

So what does all of this chemistry mumbo-jumbo mean? In simple terms, excess carbs, especially in the form of simple sugar, the EASIEST form of carbs to convert to fat, are bad. **(NO SHIT!) Stay away from too much sugar in ANY form!**

I know what you're thinking: it's OK, I've cut sugar out of my diet already…I've simply substituted one of the mass-market, non-nutritive sweeteners for sugar. Well, there is a debate there as well…nothing is EVER easy when you're dieting, and the choice of what kind of sweetener is riddled with just as many questions and concerns as any other diet topic.

On the first day, the gods of the food industry created saccharin…the "pink packet"…and fat people saw that it was good. We started putting pink packets on and in everything…coffee, grapefruit, breakfast cereal, and in our pockets when we went to restaurants…and we thought we had found the miracle cure for our collective "sweet tooth."

But then one day we were told that our beloved pink packets were causing cancer in lab rats. Forget the fact that to contract cancer from saccharin a normal human being would have to eat a bucketful of saccharin a day every day for thirty years (I may be exaggerating a bit there)… the die was cast, the health concern was made public and the fear was inserted in our brains.

So the food industry created "aspartame"…the "blue" packet"…and we turned our dieting attention to the "blue packet". The "no cancer alternative" blue packets were being sold to us at a MUCH inflated price (the philosophy being "…hey, if you want to avoid cancer it's gonna cost ya…!") and you couldn't GIVE the "pink packets" away anymore…they were now relegated to the discount aisle at the supermarket and those little packet holders in diners…if you wanted "blue packets" when you went out to eat, you had to ASK for them special and they were brought to your table on silver trays like caviar…! (another exaggeration?!)

Then one day came sucralose…the "yellow packet"…and the evil expensive blue packet had some competition again…! Finally we had a choice of non-cancer causing diet sweeteners…prices for the blue packets came crashing down and yellow packet fever spread throughout the dieting land. But, as the old adage says, "all good things must come to an end"; more studies were done that linked both the blue packets and the yellow packets to chemical processes that were rumored to be bad for our health.

So NOW what do we do? Pink packets cause cancer, blue and yellow packets have chemicals (or at least use them in the manufacturing process) that are supposed to be bad for us…accusations went flying from pink to blue to yellow and back again…prices fluctuated and them tumbled and then spiked again…a fat person didn't know from one day to another what sweetener he/she was supposed to use. Should we check the price and use the most expensive sweetener? Maybe we should check the latest scientific studies on what was most harmful to our health?

Enter the (apparent) solution: stevia, a genus of plants related to the sunflower, and currently reputed to be the ONLY all-natural (and most God-awful EXPENSIVE) non-nutritive, non-caloric sweetener currently known to man. Also known as the "green packets" to us dieters, stevia has yet to find its way to the tables of most of your finer establishments such as New Jersey diners and hoagie shops…probably attributable to its prohibitive cost (this stuff costs almost as much as gold!).

OK, OK, so we've had a little bit of fun at the expense of our sweetener friends, but how ridiculous has the war over calorie-free sweeteners been these past 20 or so years? According to the FDA, there is virtually NO DIFFERENCE between the pink, blue, or yellow packets in terms of health risks if a person uses the sweeteners in moderation and under normal conditions! Last time I checked, even the prices for all three (pink, blue, and yellow) have stabilized…making each a viable alternative to the other. In fact, the only discernible difference between the 3 sweeteners is the taste…yes, each has a distinctive flavor and aftertaste that some find objectionable…so choose your color and enjoy without fear!

Recently there has been another sweetener battle…this one among and between caloric sweeteners…the great "sugar vs. corn syrup" debate. Sugar was given a reputation as being "bad" for you because it was "empty calories." (How many times did your mom repeat that phrase when you were a kid growing up?) So we turned to corn syrup, the fructose-based (because it comes from a plant) by-product of corn. Corn syrup is a very handy and flexible product…more stable than sugar in fluids (allegedly because it is a fluid itself) so it exists better in sodas and soft drinks…and according to my mom, can even be adapted to replace more expensive products: add a little molasses and maple flavoring to it and you have a good maple syrup alternative. It is also a popular ingredient in many recipes when maintaining moisture content is important: sugar, being a dry ingredient, can absorb some moisture when it dissolves thereby making food dry…whereas corn syrup, being a liquid itself, adds moisture to a recipe.

When the sugar companies saw their sales (and profits) begin to fall, then came the inevitable anti-corn syrup claims…especially about high fructose corn syrup (HFCS). The sugar manufacturers claimed that HFCS is NOT the same as sugar…not in form (liquid vs. solid), chemical composition (sucrose vs. fructose), or the way in which our bodies metabolized the compounds. They even went as far to say that, for a certain sample of the US population, HFCS has more disadvantages than the simple "empty calories" claim. Undaunted, the corn growers responded by releasing a SLEW of advertising in support of corn syrup...unfortunately the corn proponents couldn't counter-claim against sugar since sugar already had as bad a reputation as it was going to get...the "empty calories" rep...so the corn producers went a different way with their marketing campaign. Instead of claiming that HFCS was "better" than sugar (or the inverse argument that HFCS was "less bad" for you than sugar), the corn consortium started claiming that HFCS was the "same" as sugar; pro corn syrup commercials introduced new catch phrases such as "sugar is sugar" and that HFCS was "OK in moderation" like sugar. Corn syrup producers even went so far as to apply to the FDA for permission to list HFCS as "corn sugar" on product ingredient lists, the thought being that corn "syrup" had a negative connotation, but if they could call it corn "sugar" consumers would equate it with its dry counterpart.

Of course as we all know the sugar manufacturers would not stand for that; additional research was done and submitted to the FDA for consideration in their decision-making. When ruling on the corn-grower's petition for a name change it was announced that HFCS was NOT the same as sugar and could not advertise itself that way. In fact, according to an article posted on the website cafemom (http://thestir.cafemom.com) HFCS actually poses a hazard to some who cannot metabolize it. In addition, HFCS actually boosts our fat-storing hormones…and sugar does not. Is HFCS fine in moderation? Maybe, but its residual effects can cause you more harm than its dry cousin, sugar.

OK, so sugar and corn syrup are bad for us because they have a lot of empty calories. Most if not all of the artificial sweeteners are calorie free but can be harmful because of their chemical compound or the process by which they are produced. Even honey, that delicious, naturally-occurring, sticky-sweet stuff that goes so well in tea, drizzled over pancakes, or made into wholesome candy, is questionable. **Did you know that honey is…in reality…bee vomit?** Yep, that's right…**the bee sucks the nectar from flowers like clover and honeysuckle and stores it in their stomachs for the long flight back to the beehive. After about half an hour, during which the nectar is mixing with enzymes and proteins in the bee's stomach, the bees regurgitate the newly manufactured honey into the hive for storage. YUMMY AINT IT?!**

Waitaminute...last time I had some sugar free candy (an oxymoron if I ever heard one...keep reading to see what "sugar free" really means!) I saw an ingredient called "sugar alcohol"…if it's in sugar free (from now on, I will use the abbreviation SF) candy it must be OK right? What is sugar alcohol and what does it do?

According to the website Low Carb Diets (http://lowcarbdiets.about.com) sugar alcohols (there are several) are a type of carbohydrate called "polyols." Part of their chemical structures resembles sugar and part of it resembles alcohol, which accounts for the confusing name, but there is no actual alcohol in these compounds so you can't get intoxicated by ingesting them (so far so good). They occur naturally in plants (natural...plants...still good right?) and they are like sugar in some ways, but the advantage of sugar alcohols is that they are not absorbed completely by the body like sugars (less retained calories per gram…I'm liking them more and more!). That means that you don't suffer as much from the calories in sugar alcohols as you do from the calories in sugars...which is good for diabetics and those whose blood sugar is a concern. Some to most of the sugar alcohol you consume is simply passed through your system and excreted as waste product.

Unfortunately, as you might expect with ANY substance that passes through your system without being absorbed, broken down, or processed...these compounds can cause gastrointestinal distress in the form of the aforementioned steatorrhea (loose and possibly uncontrollable stools), abdominal cramps, excessive gas, bloating, and "anal leakage."

Once again, we as consumers must make a hard choice: if you simply MUST have sugar-like substances and cannot tolerate any of the commercial artificial sweeteners, you can incorporate sugar-alcohol products in your diet…just make sure that you don't stroll too far away from a lavatory for a few hours after you eat them..!

So now we know that sugar alcohol is a misnomer: it contains neither sugar NOR alcohol…but what about REAL alcohol...? We call it booze, hooch, liquor, liquid courage, liquid lightning, spirits, and any number of other nicknames…**is alcohol good or bad for us?** Like so many products in our diets, there are organizations with commercial (and financial) agendas that make answering this question difficult. Doesn't it seem like every week we hear on the news that another research study has been done that has concluded one of two things:

1. Alcohol is good for you…in moderation of course…or

2. Alcohol is harmful to your health and should be avoided altogether

Well, I won't preach about the dangers of alcohol one way or the other…but since this is a book about obesity let's look at alcohol from a dietary perspective. Strictly speaking, **alcohol is a poison…that's right, A POISON! Ethyl alcohol, which is the kind of alcohol that we drink in beverages, is a poison.** It is metabolized by the liver…our body's natural filter…into poisonous compounds that adversely affect our ability to function. Not only that, but **ethyl alcohol has a LOT of CALORIES…just**

like carbohydrates…and these calories are EMPTY, NON-NUTRTIVE calories. That means that the calories you consume from alcohol have no nutritional value whatsoever. Need we discuss this any further? If you are obese and still need to drink alcohol, do so wisely and do so IN MODERATION.

So what do you think of when you hear the terms "fat free", "sugar free", "calorie free", or "cholesterol free"? If you're like me, you automatically think that when the word "free" is used in that context that there is ZERO amounts of whatever the food is supposed to be "free" of...in simpler terms, if the package says "sugar free", I, like the idiot that I am, assume that there is NO sugar in that product.

Uh-uh...not so fast, because believe it or not that is NOT how the FDA defines something that is "free" of a substance...in fact, according to the FDA's definitions, in NO CASE does the word "free" EVER mean completely devoid or empty of a substance...free is just another word used to signify "just a little bit"...but never nothing...! The same rule holds true for other words that the FDA considers acceptable synonyms for free, such as "zero", "no", and in some cases, even the phrase "100%." Now pardon me for asking the stupid question...or making the obvious observation...but shouldn't "100% calorie free" actually mean "zero calories"? Even worse, shouldn't something like the term "zero fat" mean NO fat...isn't that what the word "zero" means...none? Not according to the FDA it doesn't...!

For example, if you see the phrase "zero calories" on a diet soda bottle, you would expect there to be NO CALORIES in that product, but according to the FDA, a "zero calorie" soda can contain up to 5 calories per serving...so according to the FDA, 5 calories and zero calories are the same thing...welcome to the bizarro world of dieting...!

So for those of you who always wondered what "free", "low", or "reduced" meant, here are the definitions for some of the "bad" things we are supposed to monitor (or avoid) as provided by the FDA...OUR nutritional watchdogs:

Calories:

- Calorie free, zero calories, no calories: less than 5 calories per serving

- Low calories: less than 40 calories per serving...for meals and main dishes, less than 120 calories per 100 grams

- Reduced calories, less calories: at least 25% less calories per serving than an equal serving of a non-reduced serving

- Light calorie or Lite calorie: confusing here, because the FDA definition of light or lite is based not on calories but on fat; if the product contains 50% or more of its cals from fat, fat (not cals) must be reduced by 50% per serving. If the product contains LESS THAN 50% of its cals from fat, then fat must be reduced by 50% or total cals reduced by 33% per serving

Cholesterol:

- Cholesterol free, zero cholesterol, no cholesterol: Nope, not "0" mg of cholesterol as one would expect, but up to 2 mg of cholesterol per serving...!

- Low cholesterol: 20 mg or less per serving or for main dishes and meals, less than 20 mg per 100 grams. When you consider that most experts recommend less than a total of 200 mg per day for the average adult, something that is low in cholesterol can contain up to 10% of your daily cholesterol intake in one serving...!

- Reduced cholesterol: this definition is nearly meaningless, since it requires there be 25% less cholesterol in a reduced serving than is contained in a regular serving. But what good does that do a dieter when a regular serving may contain a week's worth of cholesterol.

Total Fat

- Fat free, no fat, zero fat: Less than ½ gram of fat per serving, including meals and entrees.

- Low fat: Less than 3 g per serving or 100 g in the case of an entrée or meal. Also, less than 30% calories from fat.

- Reduced fat: At least 25% less fat than a comparable food item; for example, a "reduced fat" chocolate chip cookie must have at least 25% less fat than a regular chocolate chip cookie…OR…for meals and entrees, at least 25% less fat than a regular meal of the same variety

- Miscellaneous:

  - "___% fat free" can be used if the item meets the definition of low fat; that means that ANYTHING can be labeled "99% fat free" as long as the total calories from fat are less than 30%...now you know why 1% and 2% milk are labeled that way and NOT "98% fat free" and "99% fat free"…because even though they contain only 1 and 2% fat, the total calories from fat still exceed 30%...confused yet?

  - 100% fat free can be used if the item meets the definition of fat free, which is not REALLY fat free OR 100% fat free because it can have some fat in it…what about now…confused yet?

Saturated fat:

- Fat free, no fat, zero fat: less than ½ gram of saturated fat AND less than ½ gram of trans fatty acids (trans fat) per serving…once again, no fat does not mean no fat, it means just a "little fat."

- Low fat: 1 g or les sat fat/trans fat per serving and less than 15% of total cals from sat fat/trans fat…for meals and entrees, less than 1 g sat fat/trans fat per 100 g and less than 10% total calories from sat/trans fat

- Reduced sat fat/trans fat: same as total fat, reduced

Sugar:

- Zero sugar, no sugar, sugar free: less than ½ gram of sugar or sugar containing ingredient per serving

- Low sugar: This is my favorite one…THERE IS NO DEINFITION FOR LOW SUGAR, WHICH MEANS THAT ANYONE CAN LABEL ANYTHING AS "LOW SUGAR" WITH NO REPERCUSSIONS…!!!

- Reduced sugar: Contains 25% less sugar than a comparable item…same comparison with the chocolate chip cookie: a "reduced sugar" cookie has 25% less sugar than a regular cookie.

- Miscellaneous:

  o "No added sugar" and "without added sugar" can be used on a product where no sugar or sugar ingredient was added during processing, but there is a HUGE gray area considering sweeteners such as high fructose corn syrup (HFCS)…the FDA does not include HFCS in the specific definition for "sugar ingredients", so it is possible that corn syrup could be added to products that are advertised as having "no added sugar"…since HFCS is, in fact, NOT sugar…!!

o "Unsweetened" and "no added sweeteners" are the only two phrases/terms that are defined as accurately as the words used…they mean that NO sweeteners of any kind, caloric or otherwise, were added to the product.

Sodium:

- No sodium, sodium/salt free, zero sodium/salt: less than 5 mg per serving. As a person with high blood pressure, I resent this nonsense: sodium free should mean just that…NO SODIUM…!

- Very low sodium/salt: Less than 35 mg per serving.

- Low sodium/salt: Less than 120 mg per serving or less than 140 mg per 100 g if a meal or entrée.

- Reduced sodium: Sodium content is reduced by at least 25% per serving than regular product

- Light in sodium: Sodium content is reduced by at least 50% per serving than regular product

According to the FDA (http://www.fda.gov), "natural" is loosely defined as foods that are minimally processed and free of synthetic preservatives to include:

- Artificial sweeteners, colors, flavors and other additives

- Growth hormones

- Antibiotics

- Hydrogenated oils, stabilizers, and emulsifiers

Most foods labeled natural are not subject to any government controls beyond the regulations and controls applicable to all foods; in other words, the term "natural" means little to nothing in the eyes of our government and almost any manufacturer can use it in the description of ANY of their products since there are no specific dietary guidelines that apply (thanks to the Food Marketing Institute for that information, http://www.fmi.org).

The term "all natural" is simply a made-up term by the food companies and has no bearing in reality or science…and no formal definition with respect to food, health, dietary needs, nutrition, or processing. In fact, it has been suggested that by putting the word "all" in front of the word natural actually negates the requirement to adhere to the standards of the being "natural." It has been argued by some food companies in court that "all natural" is not the same as "natural" so they should not be held to the same restrictive standards...forget for the moment that just the term "all natural" suggests a stricter code than just "natural"...YOUR FOOD COMPANIES argued that "all natural" should NOT be subject to the standards of "natural" foods...so how do you feel about 'em now??!!

The term "organic" on the other hand does have some restrictions and guidelines that apply to its use. Organic refers not only to the food itself but also to the means by which it was grown and harvested...in other words how it was produced:

- They must be certified under the National Organic Program (NOP) which took effect in October 2002.

- They must be grown and processed using techniques using organic farming methods that recycle resources and promote biodiversity.

- Crops must be grown without the use of synthetic pesticides, bioengineered genes, petroleum-based or sewer-sludge based fertilizers.

- Organic livestock must have access to the outside (and in the case of poultry only, this is known as free-range, defined below) and be given no antibiotics or steroids.

  o Free range, as defined for poultry only by the USDA, means birds that can roam freely without the restriction of cages or coops. Free range certification can be granted to birds that are allowed outside for only a portion of the day, such as to feed, but are housed protectively at night.

- They may not be irradiated in order to kill bacteria.

However, if you visit the FDA's home website and look up the definition for "organic", this is what you will find, in the EXACT words:

Query: Does the FDA have a definition for the term "organic" on food labels?

Answer: No. the term "organic" <u>is not defined by law or regulations FDA enforces</u>.

So what are we supposed to believe? If we are trying to eat healthier by buying organic, but just anyone (aka, food manufacturers) can use that term on anything they make without the threat of punitive action, how are consumers supposed to know what to do? If we rely on our government to legislate the proper use of language so that we, the consumers, know what is going into our food and how it is processed yet our government hasn't done so yet…after letting 70% of its population become overweight…what hope do we have?

Well, there you have it…the major dieting debates over "what is good for you" and "what is bad for you." I asked this once and it bears repeating: is it any wonder that our society is becoming more obese every day? Is it any wonder that so many of us give up the fight against obesity when we are being bombarded daily with conflicting information about almost every food product on the shelves? Do yourself a favor and take some advice from the author…a discouraged and confused obese consumer:

1. READ THE NUTRITIONAL LABELS on your favorite foods and choose those foods that adhere to the rules of common sense nutrition…low sugar, low sodium, sensible carbs, high lean protein, no (or at least low) fat and cholesterol

2. Eggs: when you can, use no-cholesterol or at least low-cholesterol egg substitutes but keep a dozen fresh eggs on hand for those rare times when only a fresh egg will do

3. Cut alcohol from your (and your family's) diet completely; enjoy alcoholic beverages ONLY on special occasions

4. Reduce your (family too) fat intake to zero if you can; if you can't, cut back as much as possible

5. Reduce your processed sugar intake to zero; check labels and avoid buying products with too much processed sugar. Find a non-nutritive sweetener that you like and stick to it…and ignore any research studies about the sweetener you chose

6. Unless you are passionate about products being organic, buy whatever your local supermarket has on their shelves and be happy!

Chapter 7: Being out in public

As I said before, I HATE going out in public…if you looked like me, you would too. I KNOW what people are saying about me, thinking about me, and I know most of the jokes they are TELLING about me…! Let me enlighten you to just a few things a morbidly obese person has to endure when out in public.

First let me set up some parameters for this chapter…first by considering the attitude of the non-obese public. **I did some research on my own just to prove that the general public has a generally poor opinion of obese people.** I asked the manager of a local convenience store if I could set up a table and chair outside his store to collect some opinions about obesity and obese people, and he agreed. Armed with Pez candy dispensers and some candy refills (a good researcher knows that COOL giveaways are a sure way to get people to volunteer to take part in the research and give you honest results) I planted myself outside the store with a sign that read "Answer some anonymous questions and receive a free prize." The response was HUGE…over the period of a couple of hours I collected 100 opinions from shoppers. **One of the questions I asked them was this: what is the FIRST thought that comes into your head when you see a morbidly obese person like me in public?** Here's what I learned (and they loved their Pez dispensers…old and young alike…!):

- 48% of the respondents said that they felt some measure of disgust, nausea, or were sickened by the sight of an extremely obese person…that's almost HALF of all the people asked who said that I make them sick or disgusted when they see me in public

- 32% said they felt anger or resentment…some typical responses were like "I just want to go up to them, grab them, shake them and scream at them 'Why did you let yourself get that way? Why don't you DO something about your weight? Don't you have any respect for yourself?'

- 15% said they felt sympathy or pity for the person…it should be noted that most of these respondents were themselves obese or overweight

- The remaining 5% said they were indifferent towards obese people…continuing by saying that they didn't feel obese people were worth the trouble of considering at all.

Clearly the general public has a poor opinion of fat people…you can say "they don't like us" or you can say "we're despised, pitied, and/or overlooked"…any way you say it…**normal people think less of obese people as human beings**. I can confirm this attitude from personal experience, and I'd like to share some of those experiences with you…and I'm sure that ANY morbidly or severely obese person will be able to personally relate to some of these examples as I am sure that they themselves may have experienced much the same.

First there are the STARES and the DIRTY LOOKS…the constant staring, frowning, and looks of disgust whenever I am out in public…it is one of the most uncomfortable and distasteful feelings there is for an obese person. My friends make me laugh when they claim that I am crazy when I suggest this, but that's because they are not the person being stared at…! When you are being stared at every second that you are out in public, you begin to develop a sixth sense…an ability to know…to FEEL…when everyone's eyes are on you. I call it the fishbowl effect…it's like being in a fishbowl and not being able to escape. I now know what animals in the zoo must feel like, or those unfortunate people who used to populate the side shows in the circus and carnivals…I am a walking, talking freak show…an oddity for others to stare at, whisper about, point at, and make fun of.

Some people, mostly young people, cannot limit their curiosity to a simple state. First are the children…children whose ages range from toddlers up to adolescents who I begrudgingly admit may not know any better…but it still hurts when a young boy or girl points his/her finger at me and shouts "Boy mommy (or daddy), look at how fat that guy is…!" Of course I don't blame them, and to be honest, most parents are absolutely MORTIFIED when their kids make a comment like that to me: on more than one occasion a child has been severely scolded or slapped for insulting me that way. I try to be neutral about it when the moms and dads apologize, telling them that it's OK and that I understand...the 'ole "kids say the darndest things" argument...but it still hurts.

No, the group of people who do the most hurting are the teenagers...I cannot count the number of times I have seen teenagers pointing at me...smiling at me...and worst of all...laughing at me. Of course most of them don't want me to know that I am the focus of their ridicule, so they look away as soon as I catch them, but some brave and daring souls have resorted to shouting insults...not directly AT me...just shouting "fat" insults into the thin air. When I challenge them, they play ignorant...claiming the comments were not directed at me...not meant for me...and they go away laughing with their friends, looking at me from over their shoulders until I am out of sight...imagine how proud I am...how good I feel about myself when I am treated that way.

Adults are in general more tolerant of us, but there are still whispers, smiles, and quiet hand-over-the-mouth laughs. Some bold idiots who lack a personal filter...that part of your conscience that keeps you from staying stupid, hateful, or harmful shit to others...feel the need to challenge me face to face, asking me questions like:

1. "How could you let yourself get this way?" or

2. "Don't you have any respect for yourself?" or

3. "Don't you know how unhealthy you are?" or

4. "If you don't do something soon, don't you know you could die?"or my personal favorite

5. "What's wrong with you?"

Normal people reading this book might be surprised that anyone could be that rude, discourteous, disrespectful, and abrasive, but let me tell you that while rare, it does happen. The fatter you get, the more often these assholes will approach you in public…I guess it gives them a sense of superiority to belittle a fat person in public.

I also hate the EYES…people watching me every second to see what I am doing. This is not the same as the curiosity stares or the disgusted stares I get from some folks…the EYES refers to the curiosity people have with how fat people conduct themselves in public. The worst places are the supermarket and the convenience stores…anywhere that serves or sells food. I remember years ago a particularly funny joke told by an overweight comedian: he told the story of an unkempt, dirty, scary looking man wearing a long trench coat who walked up to the check-out counter in a convenience store with a handful of particularly disgusting and obscene pornographic magazines. Behind him in line was a clean, well-dressed but morbidly obese man with a handful of candy bars; the punch line was that the OBESE man got more dirty and disgusted looks from the patrons in line…! That joke drew a laugh from the audience, but I am here to tell you from personal experience that there is a lot of truth in his description of the scene…there have been many times that I have purchased junk food at stores only to draw disgusted looks from the other customers. Grocery stores are worse, because you could have a line of 3 or 4 people behind you watching every junky, sweet, fatty, carbohydrate-filled, non-diet food product that you have chosen go by on the conveyor belt. It gets so bad sometimes that I can almost HEAR their thoughts…I know, that makes me sound paranoid and psychotic…but my hatred for going out in public combined with my hatred of the EYES creates that obsession.

One of my favorite recreational pastimes that I miss terribly yet was forced to give up when I got fat is eating out with friends. Not only do I hate the "look-at-the-fat-guy" stares that go along with going out in public, and the EYES watching me to see what I am going to order or what I am eating…or how much I am eating…I also hate worrying about every little thing that goes along with being in a crowded public restaurant. Most of these are second nature and taken for granted by the normal person, but for me they are real concerns:

1. Negotiating a tight fit: Most restaurants arrange their tables and furniture to maximize available seating. As such, there is limited room for a person to walk between tables, chairs, and around counters. An obese person often cannot get by, so unless there is a wide, unobstructed path to the table, I will inevitably bump into people or furniture during my embarrassed walk to be seated.

Also, what about seating at the table itself? Did the restaurant put 10 chairs at a table meant for a maximum of 8? Will I have enough room, or will I have to take up TWO SEATS like I do when I am on an airplane?

2. The rest rooms: Where are they? This concern is tied to the negotiating concern above (can I get from my table to the bathrooms without disturbing the other patrons?) but is expanded regarding the actual size of the rest room and whether it offers handicapped facilities. There is also the embarrassing consideration of my "special" toilet habits described earlier, but my main concern is being able just TO FIT in most public rest rooms.

3. Parking: Is the lot full, and if so, can I be dropped off at the entrance? If I am, is there somewhere I can sit until the rest of my party joins me? I HATE having to ask friends to drop me off at the door, but depending on the size of the parking lot and how far we have to walk, I NEED to be dropped off…as big as I was at my heaviest combined with my OTHER disabling condition I was able to walk only a few short yards without a rest.

4. Waiting lines: Is there a waiting line, and if so, is there somewhere I can sit that is conducive to my condition? Some places have heavy duty benches indoors or outdoors for their customers to sit on while they wait to be seated, but other establishments would rather you sit at the bar and

drink their high-priced alcohol while you wait. I don't mind this strategy, it's just good business...just don't ask a 500 pound man to sit on a high bar stool!!!

5. The furniture: This is my #1 fear...is the furniture in the restaurant durable and strong enough to support my weight?

One of the stories my friends like me to tell (in their defense they are not aware of how much it hurts for me to tell it) is of an incident that occurred at a Mexican restaurant many years ago...LONG before I was morbidly obese but well on my way. This particular restaurant had just recently opened and at the time my friends and I would get together once a week and try out different restaurants in the area...Mexican, Chinese, Italian, any cuisine was fair game. This week we had chosen this place because one of my friends had heard about their food (it was supposed to be good) and the overall atmosphere...it was supposed to be very authentic with old world furniture and a roaming Mariachi band on the premises. The place was PACKED when we got there so we were asked to wait about 30 minutes...so we decided to wait in the bar. It was equipped just as we had been told...authentic Hispanic paintings on the walls, Mexican-style furniture and artifacts decorated the place...low lighting and soft Spanish music playing in the background. The only thing that worried me were the chairs...they were very small and not made well...clearly chosen for their old-world charm but definitely NOT for their capacity to carry weight. The frames were antique wood with wicker backrests and seats.

As soon as I saw them I was alarmed…I even commented on them to my friends. We decided to sit down anyway, and as I slowly lowered my 300+ pound body in the chair I heard the telltale crack of ultimate-and-catastrophic chair failure. I barely had enough time to stand back up…in fact, I wasn't fast enough, because I was actually falling backwards and down when I grabbed the sides of the table and stood up…just in time as it turned out. The chair went down in several pieces…it looked like I had dropped a ton of bricks on it. WOW…talk about humiliating…people from several tables were laughing at me and those who missed the acrobatics were staring at me and the chair with that LOOK on their faces…that look that says "fat slob…maybe he should go home and try eating a salad instead of being here." The restaurant staff was VERY apologetic and reactive…fear of a lawsuit I would imagine…and they immediately went off to find a heavier chair for me to sit in. Note here to all restaurateurs…the gesture of fetching a fat chair for a fat person is appreciated, but it doesn't help…in fact, it makes the humiliation even worse…would YOU like to stand in the middle of a crowded restaurant, all eyes on YOU, while the staff has to fetch you a fat person chair? Why not provide adequate furniture TO EVERYONE in the first place? Anyway, my friends kept trying to tell me it was OK: "…don't worry Bill, nobody saw it happen…" (OMG…were they BLIND??!!) but the damage was done…people at the bar were already calling their friends and relatives on their cell phones to tell them of the fat guy who demolished a chair at the Mexican restaurant (I THANK GOD this happened in the days before camera phones or I would have been all over YouTube!)…people were staring…they were snickering…they were whispering…even outright laughing. I simply could NOT bear it…so I left the place….alone. My friends stayed to eat and I don't blame them for that, but I simply could not tolerate the EYES anymore…and I will never forget that night.

Furniture has become a pre-occupation in my life. As I have gotten bigger and bigger I have realized that there are only so many chairs that I can sit in. I am too big for normal steel folding chairs, and most wooden chairs that come with your average dining room set are unsuitable for me. Any chair that has attached arms is suspect; I am wider than 25 inches, which is as wide as most contemporary chairs come. Any chair too low to the ground is no good because I have a hard time lifting myself out of it, but too high and I can't lift myself high enough to sit comfortably. As I got bigger over the years and developed my other condition I found I needed deeper "support"; in other words, I needed a deeper seat to provide the support to the part of my body affected by lymph edema. I have a $2400 leather couch/loveseat combination that I haven't been able to sit on since I bought it because the seat is just too low…!

My condition deteriorated for several years before I got control of it and I had been involved in a continuous downward spiral for quite some time. When I lost my job in 2009 I immediately applied for and received handicap status in the State of New Jersey…the only advantage to this being the ability to park in those special handicapped spots. Not long after that, when it became clear that NO ONE was going to hire me in the physical condition I was in, I applied for federal disability status from the social security administration. I was a little hesitant about this: like many people on disability I felt I was giving up by applying to the federal government to support me, but I had no other choice. I was also warned not to get discouraged if I was unsuccessful when first applying; it was revealed to me that almost 80% of all first-time applicants are denied benefits. The paperwork and application process was tedious and extensive, but my doctors were very cooperative and once the administration got a look at the pre-op photos I sent along, showing the severity of my lymph edema condition, I was awarded benefits on the spot. I thank God for this program, because without it I honestly don't know what I would have done…the bariatric surgery I had in December of 2009 depleted my savings and I wasn't getting much in the way of online teaching work no matter how many resumes I sent out…so my disability income is my sole source of support. In late 2009 to early 2010, I passed what I call the "point of no return." That's what I refer to as the point when I became, for all intents and purposes, housebound. I am lucky though…I am still ambulatory (still mobile and able to get around under my own power with little or no mechanical help) and I still leave the house on occasion, but only for necessities. I don't fit in most contemporary cars, but my big 1999 Ford F250 super duty has a GIANT driver's compartment and enough room behind the wheel to accommodate me. So I can still drive to the supermarket for my weekly ½ 'n ½ and my weekly dose of stares, giggles, and finger-pointing.

"Just getting around" as I call it has become very difficult…even despite my other condition, walking has become difficult. I can't walk more than about 50 yards or so without sitting down to rest…walking around the mall or for recreation is out of the question. Without trying to invoke anyone's sympathy, just being honest…I am in pain most of the day…my legs, my ankles, my knees (I blew out my right knee last year when I stepped down wrong and now I need arthroscopic surgery on it for some ACL damage, but my insurance policy doesn't cover it) and even my wrists (from constantly pushing myself up) hurt most of the day. I have an overstuffed easy chair that has a matching ottoman and I am only completely comfortable when I am sitting in that chair…which is where I spend 23 and ½ hours every day…!

Funny thing is: being a shut in, whether it is by choice (in my case) or by necessity (as some of my bigger friends have been forced to endure) is not so bad in today's society. Many people don't realize but we have become what I like to call a "never leave home" society. From the time you are born to the day you die, if you can take full advantage of what's available in the form of deliveries and home-provided services, a person does not have to leave their home for ANYTHING, EVER. Our society now offers grocery deliveries, online bill-paying and banking services, full-service home repair and maintenance, and even SCHOOLING is available…from K-12 thru Post Grad…online. More and more employers are now offering, some even PROMOTING, telecommuting and "working from home" employment. I myself have taken advantage of this opportunity, having taught several classes to graduate business students through several online universities. If it weren't for possibly needing major medical treatment in a hospital, a person would never have to leave their house.

What I miss most are my family and friends. I won't belabor this point, because I know I will alienate my entire family if I do, but most of my family and all of my friends have all but given up on me. I am sure they will deny this…probably blame me in return for not making more of an effort to reach out to them…but the fact of the matter is this: they know I have difficulty getting around and none of them has much of an attempt to remain in touch with me. It's almost like they are just waiting for that phone call, the one telling them that I died from a heart attack in my sleep or I hemorrhaged to death from my lymph edema condition…and that call will probably be coming from my dad, who at 80+ years old is the ONLY member of my family who has made any effort to keep track of me. God Bless my dad for stopping by at least once a week depending on his schedule to check his mail and have a chat with me. Contrast that with the concern my family, all of whom I love dearly but have made NO attempt to remain in contact with me. ALL of my original family and most of my friends live less than an hour away from me…some live less than 20 minutes away…and one of them even has to pass by my house TWICE A DAY on their way to work every morning…yet none of them have made much of an effort to stay in close contact with me. _. You would think those closest to me could find time in their busy schedules to stop by once in a while to say hello and check on my condition: alas, the only family member I see on a regular basis is my dad.

My "good" friends are even worse. I have a few friends with whom I used to ride motorcycles with frequently…in fact, for a while we were riding our bikes every weekend when the weather was nice. As my condition deteriorated and I was able to do less and less, I noticed that the invites to join them diminished…to the point where I wasn't being invited out at night on the weekends at all. We still rode during the days…but as my ability to keep up with them decreased, I noticed a decrease in the invites to go riding. If the event required a lot of walking, I was left out of the ride. It all culminated during a trip me and my two friends took a few summers ago: we put our bikes in my big trailer, hooked it up to my big diesel, and drove west to South Dakota, Wyoming, and Montana to do some riding. We stopped at a lot of historical and tourist sites along the way, and when we did I would usually stay on my motorcycle while my buddies walked the attractions. I guess since then they have decided then that I am not worth hanging out with anymore...because I don't think I have been asked out once since then. In their defense however, my ability to ride ended 3 years ago after my paniculectomy operation…once my scrotum started to swell, riding became excruciatingly painful…to the point where riding was no longer enjoyable.

The time I spent with my friends went from frequent (weeknights, weekend days and nights) to infrequent (weekend days and nights) to sporadic (weekend days) to almost nonexistent (an occasional ride every now and then). For a time, as my condition continued to get worse and they noticed that I was having difficulty getting around, they would still come by the house to visit, but those visits were getting less frequent as well. When I lost my job in 2009 and my condition reached its worse point…when I first became housebound…the visits basically stopped. Two of my married friends now ignore me completely…I have lost all contact with them. Another friend who used to call me every weekend to go motorcycle riding has called me once in the past 3 years and stopped by one night for about 30 minutes. Finally, my "best" friend who I would see every weekend when I was healthy stopped finding reasons to visit me. I still get a phone call from him about once every 2 weeks or so…and he might visit for an hour once in a while if I ask him to help me out around my house (he is a GENIUS with his hands…the guy can fix ANYTHING…!) or if I have some goodies to give him like free candy (you'll read about that at the end of the book!!) or some fresh made chili…otherwise I don't see him anymore.

So what am I up to now? Well, here's what I do 24 days a day, 7 days a week. I get up from sleeping in my easy chair, have my two cups of coffee and watch TV…if I am writing something I will spend a few hours on that, if not I will check my email inboxes once or twice in the morning, but that's it. The afternoon is largely the same…TV with an afternoon meal (my ONE meal for the day) between 12 noon and 3 pm. Since I am not married and I have no children, my life has become TV and writing. As for interaction with the human race, I go out of the house once a week for milk for my coffee…so I may pass a few nice words to the check out person if they are not disgusted with me or scared to speak with me. My dad usually comes by for about 5 to 20 minutes once a week and we'll talk for a while as he checks his mail. In a normal week, that's it…if my dad decides not to stop by one week and if I bought double milk on my last trip…I will sometimes go almost 2 weeks without even opening my mouth to speak…! Try to imagine that, and you will find that you can't…FORGET VISITORS…just try to imagine not having the opportunity to even open your mouth for 2 weeks…unless you talk to yourself…! That's my life…and it has been that way for 3+ years and counting…any wonder why I am writing this book now?!

I like to end each chapter with an applicable story, so here is one that just recently occurred…so recent in fact that it was the LAST passage added to the book before I submitted it for publication. I am registered on Facebook like so many millions of us…and I am up to 135 friends (I hope to accrue millions more when this book is published!). Some of my FB friends are very good, very old acquaintances…people I have known and loved for 30 years or more. Others are people that I may have known during my life but never really got chummy with. One of these "others" posted a photo the other day and published it for all of his friends to see and comment on. It was a photo of a VERY large black man…a man who tipped the scales at somewhere in the 500+ pounds and morbidly obese range. From what I could see from the photo this man was attending a youth sporting event…Pee-Wee (aka Pop Warner) football I imagine…and he was just innocently walking to his place in the stands (maybe to the sidelines…he MIGHT have been the opposing team's coach) when the photo was snapped. So here we have this man, minding his own business, not bothering anybody, attending his son's (?) football game, when some asshole with a digital camera or cell-cam snaps a photo of him. Why was the photo taken? Just because the man was FAT…that's why! What does my so-called FB "friend" do with the photo? He posts it in FB for all of his friends to see with some sarcastic and cruel but supposed-to-be-funny caption under it like "…and for all of the women who say that size matters!" His "other" FB friends had a field day with the photo, posting cruel and hateful comments of their own in response. When I saw the photo and the accompanying comments I could not resist but to respond, giving my "friend" and his cohorts just a little piece of my mind. More on this later in this book, but is it any mystery where our children learn to be hateful and cruel to kids who are "different" when their PARENTS treat grownups this way? And what happens if this poor man's photo is shared from one friend to another? We all know how prolific sites like YouTube and FB can be…we hear all of the time about things going "viral". Imagine how proud the man in the photo will be when his co-workers post copies of his photo in his cubicle at work…or when his son or daughter comes to him crying that they are being teased at school because the picture of him is making the rounds at his/her school!

So that's what a morbidly obese person goes through…for those of you who used to watch those Discovery Health Channel shows on housebound obese people and you wondered to yourself "How can anyone let themselves get that way?"…hopefully now you know how it happens. If you have an obese friend…or just know someone who is obese AND lonely AND depressed…go visit them…or at least find out if there is an organization who can help, and have THEM send someone over to intercede. Take it from a guy who wishes someone had helped me…it will go along way…!

Chapter 8: The workplace

In the last chapter I described why I generally hate going out in public. I really do care what others think about me, and I think that anyone who claims the opposite is lying to you and themselves…don't we all desire, to some extent, the social acceptance of those around us?

There is ONE public venue that I will endure, no matter how uncomfortable it may be for me, and that is the workplace. I have always tried to be a good worker…even when assigned bad jobs. Admittedly I have had jobs that failed to challenge me or keep me busy for 8 hours a day…some that were boring at times…and some that paired me with someone that I did not enjoy working with. That having been said, overall I have enjoyed the jobs I have had in the past (almost) 30 years.

OK…so I like to work, I have generally liked my jobs, and I have usually liked the people with whom I worked…sounds like I'm a perfectly normal, well-adjusted employee doesn't it? Well think again…because there is no such thing as "perfectly normal" when you weigh 500 pounds…!

Most of my troubles occurred while I was working for my last full-time employer…because it was during that 11 +/- years that I gained most of my weight. I started that job at 250 pounds and when I left I was more than 500 pounds…averaging a whopping 25 pound weight gain per year…! I should have known that I was in trouble from the start. One of the funniest stories I like to tell was something that happened in my first or second year with the company. I was commuting from my house in New Jersey to my office in Maryland…2 hours every morning and afternoon…and since I had just started out not too many people knew about me…so work was slow. As such I wasn't traveling a lot, so I was still able to keep to a regular exercise schedule, even though it was difficult with spending 4 to 5 hours a day behind the wheel. I would drive to work in my gym clothes…shorts and tees or sweats…and I would bring my work clothes with me, a collared shirt and slacks plus a tie. There was an all-girl's college near my office and once I got to know the security force and they realized that I was NOT a pervert, they let me walk on campus in the morning, using their "loop road" as my circuit.

The problem was this: I didn't have an office, and there wasn't a bathroom big enough to change clothes in…so after my workout I had to change clothes in my cubicle…! Luckily I had a cubicle that was stuck way in the back of this four-cubbyhole network and I was mostly hidden from view…in fact, a person would literally have to come all the way around my cubby wall to see me at all. This worked out for a while…even with my 2 hour drive and my 1-2 hour walk, I was still getting to my desk by 7 am, and the office didn't open until 8:30 am…so only the real diehards were there that time in the morning.

So I would duck into my cubicle, put a pot of coffee on (I brewed my own coffee in my cubicle), and get dressed …drop my shorts, put on my pants, strip off my tee, button up my shirt, put on my tie, and I was ready for the day. This process went on for months until one day when one of the OTHER early birds decided to join me for an UNANNOUNCED and UNINVITED early morning cup of java…!

He of course HAD to be senior management, and being new he didn't know me very well yet, so that made it worse. There I was, brewing my coffee, when over the cubicle wall I heard him, let's call him "Mike", shuffling around the company coffee station…it was conveniently located just on the other side of a 6 and a ½ foot cubicle wall that formed part of my cubicle. He lifted his voice over the wall and asked me "Is that you Bill?" , to which I of course answered yes. I had my shirt on already, but had just taken off my gym shorts when I heard his voice. I didn't panic or rush to pull up my work slacks because that was all I heard from him UNTIL I heard his voice coming up the cubby walkway…I had just enough time to sit down and slide myself under my desk before he got to my cubicle opening…so my lower half was still hidden from view. What I didn't know was that he wanted to bum a cup of coffee from me…apparently the guy who made coffee for us in the morning hadn't come in yet and Mike wasn't sure how to use the coffeemaker in the kiosk. He knew I brewed my own coffee, heard my coffeemaker percolating, and decided just to bum a cup from me rather than wait for the coffee guy to come to work. My cubby was pretty deep, and I was seated on one side and the coffeemaker was behind me on the other side…which meant I had to roll my chair out from under my desk and turn around to pour Mike a cup. The rest of the story is a blur…making apologies, I know I made several of those…me trying to explain about trying to get some exercise…and how I had nowhere to change…Mike suggesting that I join the local Bally's which was less than 100 yards down the street..and Mike smiling. The best part of that story was the fact that Mike and I became good friends…in fact, despite what the REST of senior management thought of me, Mike was always one of my biggest advocates…he really appreciated what I brought to the table for the company and never took me for granted. But aside from his other fine qualities, the one attribute that made Mike stick out from the rest of senior management was his compassion: he never thought less of me because of my weight…a quality that was NOT shared among the other officers in the company. He died tragically a few years ago and I will miss him forever. They don't make guys like Mike anymore. If the world had more folks like Mike in it, I probably wouldn't have had to write this book…!

Obesity acceptance in the workplace is not easy. First of course an obese employee must overcome the typical stereotypes about obese people discussed earlier in this book. It's hard to do when you are simply passing someone in the street or in a supermarket: they don't know anything about you except what they see with their eyes, so whatever stereotype they affix to you or opinion they form about you, you're pretty much stuck with it…you can't do much about how people think…and you can't legislate opinions. However, give me a few minutes with a person and I can dispel some if not all of those preconceived notions about fat people and the limitations that the public think we possess. Within minutes I can convince anyone that I am lucid, I'm smart, I'm capable, I'm not lazy or stupid, I don't smell (I shower every day AND use cologne), and

I'm generally a nice guy with a KILLER sense of humor. Most people like me after they get to know me.

Picture perfect scene, right? Not hardly, because despite their best intentions, most people simply cannot be themselves around a morbidly obese person. First of all there is the fish bowl scenario #2: the inevitable stares and whispers. Sitting in a cubicle I invariably receive stares from everyone who passes by my station…they can't help it. I am a freak show to them…a zoo exhibit…some weirdo who is not like other people…oh sure they won't admit it, but that's how they all feel. When there is a 500 pound man sitting in a cubicle exposed to everyone…someone who doesn't look like ANYONE else they know…a person just has to LOOK.

Interaction with clients is especially hard; in many cases my past employers would not even introduce me to the clients until AFTER we had an executed contract with them. My employers were apparently afraid that my size might have a detrimental effect on the company's image and might lessen our chances of securing the contract or project we were pursuing…so I was hidden from view until it was too late. Going back to the opinions and stereotypes that people form about fat people, if the client, through no fault of their own, assigned any of those unfavorable qualities to me as a team member and then as an extension assigned the stigma of "poor judgment" to my company for having me on staff, it could have meant a significant reduction in our workload. I can't count the number of presentations, client interviews, and sales calls I was left out of…when it was CLEAR that under normal circumstances a person of my expertise would have been an asset to the team's overall structure and capabilities. No explanation was ever given for omitting me from these opportunities…but I am smart enough to know what people think of me…so I simply never challenged the decisions.

In several cases I was even hidden from the client's view unless it became absolutely necessary to introduce me; I imagine that in these cases it might look bad for the team if it was revealed to the client that one of the team's experts was a fat man unless his expertise was cooking or eating…! Imagine a client who feels that obese people in general are incapable of accomplishing anything of responsibility; what is that client going to think if they are told that a 500 pound person is in charge of the timely completion of their multi-million dollar construction project? What kind of confidence will they have in the company doing their work?

So I led a pretty solitary life at my last job…I had a few friends with whom I enjoyed hanging out…but even with regards to them, I honestly don't know what they truly thought of me. When I first started that job and my weight was still mostly within control I would eat lunch with one of my friends or go down to the lunchroom/deli that was located in the building. Then, as I started to grow, I found that I didn't enjoy eating in front of anyone, even my friends. I would eat my lunch alone in my cubicle with my back to the cubicle opening so no one could see me eat or see what I was eating…and at the very end of my tenure with that company, I would go down to my truck parked in the dark underground garage and eat my lunch there. I just wanted to get away from those prying and curious eyes when I ate.

I smile when I think back to the way some people treated me back then. The one group that made the biggest impression on me was single females…they were PETRIFIED of me…! You see, when a guy gets fat, he becomes, for lack of a better term, a eunuch. Women begin to see us as "sexless"…a man without a penis…we become "safe"…we no longer represent a threat to their womanhood. We become that male "friend" that every woman like to have…a guy who they can tell ALL their intimate secrets to, because no matter how sexy, erotic, or downright pornographic they get, we are expected to be neutral and unemotional…we have no sexual organs, remember? If you don't have a penis, you won't get excited or have an erection…so they can tell us ANYTHING…! I spent an entire 11 miserable years as the "safe" friend to dozens of women…! There is NOTHING more emasculating to a man than to be considered the "safe" friend to a hot, sexy, single woman.

However, once a single guy gets above a certain weight…the single woman's opinion of him changes. No longer is he safe…he becomes dangerous…a predator…a molester…a pervert. I honestly don't know what comes over women when a man gets really fat…maybe it's the combination of several stereotypes working at once…she is disgusted with him, she sees him as a pervert…so she develops a loathing for him. What's more, the exact OPPOSITE transition seems to occur in married women…they generally seemed more accepting of me as I got fat. But the single women…they avoided me like the plague.

I called it the "fear of being nice" syndrome. Single women were afraid to be nice to me for fear that I might interpret their intentions incorrectly. This was doubly insulting because not only were they insulting me as a man but they were also insulting my intelligence: apparently they didn't think I was smart enough to know the difference between a woman who is simply being courteous and a woman who is flirting. Furthermore, I was also smart enough to know what "league" I was playing in: when you are a 500 pound man, you would have to be a moron to think that you are in the same league as a hot, sexy, single woman.

Most of the single women avoided me whenever they could. I would try to pass neutral pleasantries in the morning or when I saw them at the coffeemaker or in the hallways, but usually all I got for my troubles was a barely discernible smile or a look-the-other-way. Some of them were SO scared of me that they went out of their way to avoid me, crossing the hall or ducking in a doorway so as not to encounter me...or my favorite move, when a woman would walk YARDS out of her way just to avoid passing by my cubicle…some women would literally walk the other way just to ensure no interaction with me…!

So except for the women, most of my co-workers accepted me, or at least tolerated me. Being as big as I am there are so many things that I have to worry about that normal sized people take for granted…furniture for example. In an earlier chapter I spoke about being wary of furniture when I would go to a restaurant to eat, well the same thing happens in most office scenarios as well…sometimes with unfortunate circumstances. For example, most restaurants buy commercial furniture for their establishments in order to avoid any possible accidents. The chairs are rugged and durable and MOST anyone can come in and sit on them without a care. Not the same holds true for office furniture…especially on a construction project that is on a budget…!

I first started to worry about furniture after destroying that flimsy wooden and wicker chair at the local Mexican restaurant…yes, just like Gwyneth Paltrow's character did in the movie "Shallow Hal". So from that point on I had to consider where I sat whenever I was out of the office. When I started back in 1998 I was allowed to choose my own office chair and I chose one that was a little "wider" than usual but still fell within the parameters of being considered a "normal" piece of office furniture; that being the case, my company didn't have to spend too much more for my chair than one of the generic chairs that they purchased in bulk. By the time I hit 400 pounds or so, the time had come for me to get a new chair. The chair I started with in 1998 was all but destroyed: it now leaned precariously to one side, none of the pneumatic controls worked (up/down, back recline, or seat angle), and one of the casters was creaking ominously. My supervisor at the time was great about my needs; he allowed me to purchase a desk chair specifically designed for a "large" person…wider and deeper in the seat, armrests spaced generously apart, heavy duty casters and higher in the back. I LOVED my chair…!

The only problem was that I couldn't take my chair with me everywhere I went. When I visited a jobsite or a client's office I was at the mercy of whatever furniture they had on hand. Even within the walls of my own company I had to be wary…I remember being called down to one senior VP's office for a consult and carefully sitting in his high backed wooden guest chair. As soon as I started lowering myself into it I knew there was going to be trouble; the armrests were spaced so close together that I couldn't get my butt to fit between them. Remember that scene in Eddie Murphy's version of "The Nutty Professor", when Eddie's character is called to the dean's office and he gets stuck in the chair? Now you can envision what was going on in the senior VP's office…I finally seated myself and as I sat back I heard one of the armrests crack…never did find out if the VP heard it too, but I immediately sat forward again to avoid breaking both armrests completely.

There were other instances as well, too many to list here. I broke or permanently disabled dozens of folding chairs (did you know that folding chairs are weight-rated from 200 lbs for the cheaper ones up to 300 lbs for the better ones…but if you want "recumbent" folding chairs, rated all the way up to 500 or even 600 lbs, you will pay a PREMIUM price for them…!) and several rolling chairs…the most common failure was the casters. When I would sit on the chair and try to roll around, the casters would crack or simply collapse under my weight.

The most memorable and humiliating experience I had with office furniture occurred (luckily for me) in the home office of the company. It was around the same time I destroyed the wooden chair in the Mexican restaurant, so my furniture radar was still developing…! I chose to sit in a chair that was supported by a single continuous piece of light gauge chromed steel. The primary problem with this piece of furniture was the way it supported itself: not only was the support steel's structural integrity questionable, it supported only the front half of the chair. There was nothing supporting the back half of the chair…so if an unsuspecting fat person were to lean back….

…which was exactly what I did. I sat down and positioned my weight towards the front of the chair…this pose was typical for me, as I needed to be sitting forward if I wanted to take notes during a meeting. However, when the meeting slowed and one of the presenters was discussing a topic that was not in my job description, I decided to lean back. Suffice to say, I crimped the two steel uprights like they were made of cardboard…when I leaned back, the chair's support system didn't stop me…I just kept going back, back, and back…all in all it was a slow and gentle failure…until I found myself sitting on the floor in front of a roomful of people staring at me and smiling. Rack up another humiliating personal experience for the fat guy on the 10th floor…!

Clothing was another consideration: it's one of those worries that non-obese people take for granted. Take traveling for example: if a normal sized person loses their luggage on a flight across the country all they have to do is find the nearest department store and buy new clothes. It may be a minor inconvenience but not a catastrophe. To the obese person however clothes that fit our bodies are not available at every store; in fact, the bigger you are, the less places exist that stock clothes that fit you. Not every town and city that we visit on our business travels has a Lane Bryant (for the women) or a Casual Male Big and Tall (for the guys). Because of my physical condition I have been reduced to shopping at a pitifully few "big and tall" websites that stock clothes for the super (morbidly) obese male…imagine if MY luggage were lost on a flight! Where am I going to go to get replacement clothes in a pinch?

One particularly funny thing happened to me while on a business trip a few years ago. I was required to attend a meeting with a potential client…one of the few times that my company found it necessary to "expose" me to a client before the work had been secured. When we were escorted into the room where the meeting was to occur there were several empty rolling office chairs available so each of us…my company team members…sat down in the nearest chair to us. Unfortunately for me the chair that I chose was adjustable and had been lowered to its lowest setting by the person who occupied it before me. When I lowered myself into the chair I heard a low sharp tearing sound: ***the seat of my pants had just ripped up the seam, from crotch to waistband!*** I was MORTIFIED!! I tried to contain my embarrassment and humiliation throughout the meeting because it seemed, to my luck and good fortune, that I was the only person who had heard the "catastrophic failure" of my pants! (Catastrophic failure is a term we construction folks use to describe when a structure fails due to overloading of the weight bearing members…very appropriate in my case!) Lucky for me when it came to my turn in the presentation I wasn't required to get up to make my sales pitch…and when the meeting ended, I notified a good friend of mine (who was ALSO at the presentation) what happened to my pants. He was nice enough to walk behind me all the way back to the car, down the streets of Baltimore Maryland, so that my underwear would not show out the back of my torn pants!

Overall I really can't say that any employer has ever denied me anything due to my disability. When it came to traveling my last employer let me drive my company car if the cost was reasonable rather than flying. When I HAD to fly, they were great about letting me buy a 1st class ticket so I could get the "big chair." I remember with mixed feelings the looks of fear and worry from the other passengers when I was sitting in the terminal waiting to board the plane…in some cases I even had people come up and ask me what my seat number was…presumably so if I was seated next to them they could change their seat assignment before boarding. Of course NO ONE wants to be stuck sitting next to the "fat guy", especially if I was booked in a middle seat, my biggest flying nightmare. Before I started flying 1st class, when I was big but not REAL BIG yet, I would walk down the aisle of the airplane and people would actually look away and ignore me…as if ignoring me would make me go away…or as if looking at me was bad

174

luck…bad mojo…and if they looked away it would bring them good luck so they wouldn't have to sit next to me…! There were the inevitable unhappy sighs, eye-rolling, and under-the-breath complaints from the unfortunate passengers who got stuck next to me…and the embarrassment as everyone stared at me while I tried to SQUEEZE myself between the armrests of the seat. Then came the added humiliation of having to ask the stewardess for a seatbelt extension because the regular seatbelts were not long enough to go around my waist. Did you know that those little seatbelts that are used during the safety demonstration have a dual role on the airplane? They are ALSO used as the seatbelt extenders for fat people…! I did a lot of flying on US Air and particularly back and forth to Orlando Florida for about a year. I took the same flight from Baltimore to Orlando every Monday morning for a while, so I got to know the normal Monday crew for that flight quite well. One particularly kind and understanding stewardess named Angela (I hope she reads this and remembers me…!) did me a BIG favor one morning…I was seated next to the worst fat-bigot I ever met…started complaining about having to sit next to me from the first second I sat down. At first he just LOUDLY announced that he wanted to change seats…saying that he didn't want to "…get stuck sitting next to this guy for 2 and a ½ hours…" pointing to and referring to me of course. When the stewardess notified him that the plane was booked solid…he actually argued with the stewardess for everyone to hear how he wanted a refund for his ticket. He felt that he deserved a reasonably comfortable flight for the money he paid, and he was NOT going to get it stuck next to a fat guy like me…I'm paraphrasing of course, but ALMOST his exact words…! Then came the agonizing exercise of having to ask the stewardess for my seat belt extension, but almost as if she was reading my mind, Angela was there with my extension…she quietly and secretly handed it to me with a wink so as not to raise anymore rude comments from my seat neighbor. When we landed, I carried my seatbelt extension up the aisle with me as I deplaned, as was customary…but when I got to the front of the plane Angela met me and whispered in my ear "Why don't you just hold on to that strap for next time?" With another wink and a smile I thanked Angela and deplaned…and even though I lost touch with her, I still have that strap and I will never forget her kindness…!

Not only did my former employer accommodate my furniture and traveling needs, they also accommodated my personal hygiene needs: they put a handicapped unisex bathroom near me when I was on the 9th floor and then again in the hallway near my cubicle when I was moved to the 10th floor. Of course one of the most obvious examples of obesity discrimination in the workplace is being denied promotions or raises due to a disability. The difficult part of this argument, as is the case with ANY discrimination or equal opportunity complaint, is PROVING that the company discriminated against you for the obvious reason…and I can't do that either. I feel that I did the best I could while working for my last employer…I gave them everything I had, putting in 12 and 14 hour days for no extra money…going everywhere they asked me to, even when they knew that traveling in any form was difficult for me. At the end, when traveling just became too much for me, I devised ways to adequately accomplish my job without traveling, utilizing technology and working during my off hours to get the job done. Despite all this, I was passed over for promotions time and time again, and I basically left the company at the same place in the company hierarchy as when I arrived. At the end, all I got for my 11 years of hard work was a simple "Bill, it's just not working out for us…" and a goodbye. I was escorted out of the building that very same day and I never returned.

But why should I worry…I had achieved my PhD just 2 months earlier and I was planning a career move anyway, so the timing for this "speed bump" was perfect. NOW I could concentrate on getting that teaching job that I had been dreaming of for years. What I didn't know, and I will admit to a great deal of ignorance and naivety here, was that NOBODY wants to hire an obese person. My chances of securing another job as an obese applicant were slim, no matter how good my credentials looked. I have spoken to a few employers about this subject and most claim that they would NEVER discriminate against an obese person: if two people are being considered for an opening, and one is normal sized while the other is obese, both have an equal chance of securing the position. Now, that's what they CLAIM…now here's the truth.

Obese applicants have an 80 to 90% less chance of being hired than their normal sized counterparts. In fact, studies have shown that in many cases a "lesser qualified" normal-sized person will be hired for a job rather than a "better qualified" obese person. Some of the reasons for this discrimination, as provided anonymously by hundreds of employers participating in the survey, are as follows:

1. Obese employees cost too much: sadly this urban legend is all too true. Health insurance for an obese person can cost upwards of TWICE what similar insurance would cost for their normal-sized counterpart

2. Obese people have too many restrictions/limitations: sadly this is also true. We have difficulties traveling and may have special needs with regards to furniture, entrance and exit ways, and lavatories (see my story about the exploding toilet in an earlier chapter!)

3. Obese people tire too easily: this one is a stereotype, but there is some truth to it. If a job requires a significant amount of physical exertion, the obese employee may tire sooner than their peers

4. Obese people do not meet our corporate image: in some cases this is a legitimate grievance. I would have to concede that companies such as Hooters or Chippendales would not have succeeded half as well had they allowed obese men and women in their ranks. However, this argument's legitimacy is harder to prove in cases where body image is NOT a primary job requirement. For example, consider the next argument…

5. Our clients do not have as much confidence in obese employees as they do in normal sized employees: this was a popular criticism among employers, and let's face it, a hard one to argue. When an organization's

reputation and financial well-being hinge on what the client thinks of it as a whole, any factor that detracts from that reputation needs to be eliminated. A GOOD leader will argue in favor of his/her employees regardless of their size, but when faced with a customer who is an obese-bigot the employer must err on the side of what's good for the company, not the single employee.

6. Obese people are anti-social; they are angry and have no senses of humor: another stereotype, but allow me to submit that when treated like I was by the single women in my last job is it any wonder that I am angry and anti-social? Maybe it was not appropriate of me to return disdain with disdain, but after many attempts to win those women over it became a discouraging battle. I'm not sure about the sense of humor criticism, but instinct tells me that the humor being referenced may have been humor at the expense of the obese person…and NOBODY likes to be made fun of.

The bottom line is this: discrimination in the workplace mirrors discrimination by the population. What people think of the obese PRIVATELY they will think of them PROFESSIONALLY as well.

Chapter 9: Our kids and school

The group that suffers from obesity the most is, of course, children. They represent the group least capable of protecting itself. I'd like to start this chapter by TRYING to put this dilemma into perspective for those of you who don't know what it's like to be ridiculed, scorned, humiliated, harassed, and bullied.

Elsewhere in this book I try to describe what it's like to be an obese shut-in…how I can go sometimes two weeks without human contact of any kind…and it goes beyond just not SEEING anyone…I mean not speaking to anyone…to the point of not having ANY reason to even open my mouth for weeks at a time. I tried to describe what it feels like to have no interaction (except maybe electronic, if one of my Facebook friends contacts me) with anyone for long periods of time…the loneliness, the depression, the boredom…all emotions which serve to AGGRAVATE and worsen the eating disorder that caused them in the first place! However, when I try to describe these feelings to someone in person the actual severity of the condition is lost…everyone THINKS they know what it's like…they nod their heads and say "yes, I've been there before, I know where you're coming from" because maybe once, for a day, they were stuck inside their home with the flu and had no visitors for a few hours. Sorry folks, NOT the same thing: until you can say that you had that same flu and no one who cared enough to come by to check on you for 14 days STRAIGHT, then you do NOT know what I am talking about!

The same thing, sadly, is true about trying to describe the misery overweight kids go through every day in school in terms that the average person, who WASN'T bullied in school, can understand. The best I can do is this: think back to your MOST embarrassing experience…maybe you went out of the house missing a piece of clothing, maybe someone caught you doing something you weren't supposed to do, maybe you got drunk at an office party and Xeroxed your butt on the copying machine and passed out copies only to have everyone paste them up in their cubicles the next day. Think back to how you felt that day: the embarrassment and humiliation; the fear of punitive action or retribution; the desire to go home and avoid your co-worker's eyes, their snickers, the outright laughs and jokes at your expense, and the finger-pointing. All you could do during the aftermath was endure, wishing it was over and counting the minutes until that time came.

Now take that feeling and multiply it, exponentially, to include every minute of every day, five days a week and sometimes six, for 12 years or more. Your "moment" lasted what…a few hours? A few days? Maybe a week? If it was REALLY embarrassing, maybe a few months? Well, if your children are the targets of cruel and insensitive kids at school, their "moment" lasts their entire school life…! They are living what you lived but not for a moment…rather, they live it every day they go to school.

So now imagine this: your kid is overweight and too embarrassed to tell you about it or seek help, so they suffer in brave-but-miserable silence. Here's how their day MIGHT go:

They wake up and it begins…they may still be thinking about whatever they endured the day before, or maybe are feeling some anxiety from a threat leveled at them by the bully they encountered at the end of the day yesterday…a promise to get beat up for their lunch money, or to have shit thrown in their face just for fun, or to be pantsed (in the vernacular, to be "pantsed" means to have your pants pulled down in front of a group of laughing kids) or the victim of a wedgie at lunchtime. Maybe they are lucky…maybe it's a new day and they meet it with a renewed sense of hope that maybe TODAY those kids at school will finally stop tormenting them.

So they look in their closet for something to wear and the memories flood back, drowning any thoughts or hopes of redemption for the day: the SAME clothes they have worn in the past, and the same clothes for which they have been repeatedly ridiculed in days gone by. Most clothing manufacturers, even those who specialize in clothes for children and young adults, do not extend their lines to include the "overweight" children in those categories. Parents of overweight kids are forced to shop at the few manufacturers who have "special" lines of clothes designed for "robust" children…admittedly, I did not do my research in this area, so I don't know which manufacturers offer clothes for overweight kids, but what I DO know from having spoken to a lot of overweight children is this: the clothes are there, but they are NOT the stylish, modern, fashionable clothes that the "cool" kids wear. Clothes for overweight kids tend to be more "functional" than fashionable, more "durable" than designer, and more "sturdy" than stylish. When I was a kid I remember doing my back-to-school shopping out of a Sears catalog because it was the only clothing manufacturer that had a "husky" line (and to this day, I seethe with hatred and resentment when I hear that word used…!). My poor mom had to order "husky" pants for me and then hem the inseam several inches because my waist was MUCH bigger than my inseam was long; a big belly and short legs, my lifelong curse…! Anyway, I grew up in the seventies, the decade of disco, so while my classmates were wearing their polyester shirts and pants (and as we have learned, NOT a very popular fashion statement in itself, but that was what we were wearing back then!) I was stuck wearing hemmed corduroy and flannel shirts from the Sears catalog. My male friends looked like Travolta from "Saturday Night Fever" and I looked like a lumberjack from a Monty Python episode…! I had the Python "Lumberjack Song" sung to me so many times back then that I can STILL remember the words to this day…!

So your kids are dressed and they are sick with anxiety thinking about the taunts, insults, and physical abuse they will receive just because of their clothes…so they overeat at the breakfast table. This is part of the vicious cycle that the overweight person must endure 24 hours each day…the anxiety of being overweight drives their desire to eat, making the condition worse. In the case of your children, imagine their young and impressionable minds being FILLED with worries about the torment they are about to endure…and being filled with these worries for the entire time they are awake and conscious…! The anguish gets so bad for them that they get to the point where they can't think about anything else…their minds are constantly preoccupied with the thoughts of what they must endure at school. If you're the parent of an overweight child, is the hopelessness and despair your kids are feeling STARTING to sink in now? If you're the parent of a bully, or one of the "other" kids who are cruel, disrespectful, insensitive, intolerant, and unwilling to accept overweight kids as just KIDS…I hope you too are beginning to see what kind of damage your kids are doing to others in school…!

Getting to school is an obstacle course…a series of people and places to avoid in order to prevent conflict…if your obese kids are as observant as I was when I was young, they learn quickly the best routes to and from school to avoid bullying. When I was in grade school, there was one bully in particular who had his evil sights set on me…let's call him "Eddie." He despised me and this friend of mine (we'll call him Jay)…we were both "portly" and Eddie decided that Jay and I would be his targets. Eddie even had special insulting names for me and Jay…which I won't divulge so as to keep their real identities anonymous…let's just say he wasn't convinced of our masculinity…! Anyway, Eddie and his friend would follow me and Jay around every chance they could get, but recess after lunch was his favorite time. Jay and I would try to find a quiet corner of the playground to relax or to participate in whatever sport was active at the time, but invariably Eddie would find us and the torment would begin…name calling, physical threats, insults, slander. One day as we walked back to classes after recess, Jay, Eddie, his friend and I were all in the back of the pack and Eddie was in particularly good form that day…hurling insult after insult at Jay and me…and finally I snapped…! He was standing directly behind me and without looking I spun around and smacked him across the face with my left hand…I can't really call it a punch since I don't think my fingers had formed a fist, but it was enough of a shot that it snapped Eddie's head back. Well, he recovered quickly and was on me in a flash, jumping on my shoulders and proceeding to beat me in the back of the head for several minutes. When he was finished he actually threatened to kill me…mind you this is circa 1973 and we were 7th graders; the violence that permeates our schools today was not an issue back then, but he actually threatened to kill me with a knife after school. Of course I was petrified and was worried sick all the rest of the day…and when the school day ended I have only flashes of memory about my walk home that day (I lived too close to school at the time to be eligible for bus transportation). I remember waiting in school for at least 30 minutes (I didn't know that Eddie took the bus and was already gone…all I could remember was his threat to kill me) checking all of the exits for signs that Eddie might be outside waiting for me. Once outside, I took back roads, used backyards when I could, backtracked several times to confuse anyone who might be following me, and finally getting home around dusk…much to the displeasure of my parents. I actually don't remember how the tale ended…whether I told my dad about Eddie and he took care of it for me (my dad was a pretty important guy in the school system…the "big boss" you might say) or if Eddie just got tired of taunting me and found another victim…but I do know that not long after the punching incident he left me and Jay alone for the rest of the year…and in an ironic twist ending to the story, Eddie was held back at least one year, so for the rest of my school life he was behind me in class year…which helped keep him out of my way most of the time.

So your kids are in school now; imagine all the fears and anxiety they have suddenly come to life and find a voice…or better stated…MANY voices…! Rude comments, insults, ridicule come at them from every direction. Even the kids who may be in one of the OTHER bullied groups…the "geeks", the "brains", the "weird" kids…are no help. They are sadly comforted that, at least for the moment, THEY are not the current targets of this barrage of cruel treatment, so they just sit there…ignoring your kids as if they weren't even there. If your child is overweight, it is conceivable they may not have one, single, solitary ally in their plight.

The misery doesn't stop at the verbal…there will invariably be the physical abuse from the bigger bullies…those kids who were brought up by parents who believed in "do unto them before they do unto you" and "life is a jungle kid…survival of the fittest…a dog eat dog world out there." These kids grow up thinking that it's fun to pick on the weaker or weirder or different kids…they get some cheap thrill out of the experience. Their parents might think it's "cute", dismissing the behavior as "youthful exuberance" or "just a phase they'll grow out of." Maybe, and this is almost too horrifying to suggest, but just maybe they are PROUD of their kids for being the bullies…! Fathers are proud of their sons for being "tough and strong", and mothers are proud of their daughters for being at the top of the "popular crowd"…the "alpha kid" syndrome.

So your kids are forced to suffer this scenario for 6, 7, 8, or 10 periods a day. Every class offers a new misery or a different kind of torment…maybe from several directions at once. In fact, the only time an overweight kid is spared the suffering is during class lectures, but it is likely that even during lectures your kid's mind is reeling with thoughts of the misery that has already happened or what is to come.

I hope you're not already tired of reading my lengthy description about the suffering an overweight child endures at school…I am spending an inordinate amount of time on this topic because, as I stated at the beginning of this chapter, I want ALL of you to try to get just a small idea of what overweight children go through at school. No matter how well I may put their experiences into words it PALES in comparison to what the kids actually endure. I could try to enhance your appreciation by using some literary tricks like repetition, where the author repeats the same statement, concept, or thought over, and over, and over again simply for emphasis…it's a VERY effective technique, and would be especially effective in this case. I think describing a single, individual case of bullying may be poignant and might strike a nerve with the reader, but describing it countless times, equaling the number of times your overweight children must endure the same during the average school day, would be heartrending. I COULD do that, but I think it would be better to leave that to your imagination…if you're a smart person, you now have enough information to make your own conclusions about school bullying. However, I would not be doing this topic justice if I failed to discuss the worst two periods of the day for the overweight student: lunch and gym class.

Lunch is the easy one…maybe even the less distressing, since it is the one period of the day where an overweight kid can retreat to the only place where they may feel comfortable: the world of food. I was a fat kid up until my last 2 years in high school, and I was bullied relentlessly, especially during lunch. The bullies, usually the older guys, would bother me during the entire lunch period…following me no matter where I sat in the lunchroom. Yes, even back in the 70's the lunchroom was separated into "cool tables" and the "reject tables." The cool tables consisted of the jocks, the stoners, the shop-classers, the A-listers, and in MY school even the "brainiacs." The rejects included the geeks, the weaks, the weird, and everybody else. Unfortunately the fat kids had nowhere to go since they didn't fit in with anyone else…and there weren't enough of us to form our own group. So I would "roam" the lunchroom until I found a single seat at the end of an uncool table where I could sit by myself. If I was lucky I would go unnoticed by the bullies and I could eat my lunch alone and in silence…but that didn't stop "the EYES." I could FEEL them on me as I ate…kids from every clique in school watching the fat kid eat…and to add insult to injury, even long pathetic stares by some of the teachers…!

If I was unlucky, someone would notice me and they would approach me…insults and name calling were the norm…the standard…let's call it the "mildest" form of lunchroom torture I would endure. On especially BAD days I would get asked for my lunch money, even though it was clear that I no longer had it since I had a school lunch sitting in front of me. On a personal note, I never knew what those guys were thinking…what was their agenda? Were they REALLY that stupid that they didn't realize that the lunch in front of me was proof that I no longer HAD my lunch money? Were there hoping that I was carrying MORE money that they could take just for spite, or were they practicing for their future careers in theft and crime?

After the obligatory physical abuse that followed my admission of being penniless…"I don't have my lunch money anymore guys"…then a hard slap to the back of the head, a set of knuckles to my forehead, maybe a skull crack with a class ring turned around on a finger, maybe a wrist burn…that would be the balance of the torture…NOTHING in comparison to what kids go through nowadays. Invariably it meant I wasn't going to get to eat ANY of my lunch…whatever the bullies wanted from my tray they took, sometimes they ate it, sometimes they used the food to decorate me. All the while, during these sessions, they would lecture me on how they were doing this for my own good…telling me that I was fat and I ate too much anyway, so missing a meal or two would be GOOD for me…and I should thank them for helping me become thinner. I'll never forget one particularly harsh session during my freshman year where I was brutalized by a group of senior football players…at the end I was wearing my sloppy joes in my lap, mixed vegetables were in my hair, my milk was in my shorts, and the football players were eating my dessert and my french fries. To top it all off, they wanted me to thank them, one at a time and loud enough so everyone within earshot could hear me. It was then that the head football coach walked up to the table and asked what was going on…and with a straight face, they all lied and told him that they had just RESCUED me from a bunch of guys who were harassing me. I tried to object and tell the coach the truth, but one of them had me in a head lock and was making me smell the bench of the lunch table, so he simply tightened his grip on me. I got the message and kept my mouth shut. When they were asked about the headlock they admitted that they were trying to get me to thank them for their help and I was being an asshole about it when the coach walked up. Of course the coach believed them and even made me thank them for their help (although to his credit he did make them release me from the headlock) before he made them disperse.

Gym class is an entire chapter unto itself, and I won't go into the infinite scenarios of torture and torment that an overweight kid could endure in gym class and even worse, the LOCKER ROOM. Let me set it up by reminding you of YOUR school experience with gym class and then I will leave what COULD happen to your imagination. Gym class is a place where:

- Kids have to undress, and in high school this includes undressing to the point of full nudity as many schools require boys to wear athletic supports. Unless you wear it under your clothes when you leave the house, this means you have to put it on before class.

- Kids have to participate in physical activities with equipment; some of it so dangerous where it can almost be compared to weapons...anyone else see the movie "Balls of Fury"?

- Kids have to take, in many cases, group showers. In the old days we had the towel snappers...guys who would wet a towel, roll it up, and then snap it on the butt of an unsuspecting victim, leaving a red welt that would sting for hours. The abuse nowadays is much worse and includes the worst criminal activity imaginable: things that we envision only happen in jails, like rapes, sodomizing, and even hangings

- There are toilets...where bodily waste is deposited and oft times not sent through the sanitary system that services the facility by the person doing the depositing...in other words, there is urine and shit in the toilets, left there by kids who didn't flush...and I don't need to tell you what THAT can lead to in the group showers, do I?

- There are no teachers immediately available in the locker rooms, unlike the classroom where the teacher is always within view

- The teachers who are in charge of these classes...the "gym teachers"...might themselves have been bullies at one time or another...their sympathy for the unfortunate kids in their classes is limited

- The teachers who are in charge of these classes are largely "coaches" for the major sports teams in the school…the teams with the greatest concentration of bullies in the school…so their protection is extended more to their players than the victims (case in point: my lunchroom example above)

So why aren't the SCHOOLS doing something about this then? If abuse and behavior like this is going on in our public schools, why isn't there a system to protect our kids? I think the answer to that question is twofold…and I'm going to piss off a lot of people with my theory, but I don't care…the answer is part discrimination and part legal.

First the legal answer: our schools are required to protect ALL of our kids, not just the unfortunate ones, and our judicial system was born on the premise of "innocent until proven guilty." When it becomes one kid's word against another's, there is a stalemate…school administrators can't show favoritism even if the one being accused has a record of such abuse. In fact, as ridiculous as it may sound, a school administrator could find themselves on the wrong end of a lawsuit for even correcting or disciplining an accused student for behavior that can't be verified.

When there is a clear cut case of bullying, there is only so much a school can do to the perpetrator. Most schools don't have guidelines regarding punitive discipline for bullying so many initial cases are settled verbally or with minimal punishment like a session of detention. In more drastic cases or in the case of a repeat offender a school may choose to invoke a temporary suspension from school. However, the ultimate punishment of permanent expulsion from school is considered only in the most severe cases of behavior…and sadly your garden variety non-injurious bullying does not reach that extreme. It's simply just not considered a severe-enough anti-social behavior to warrant kicking the offending party out of school.

Now the discrimination answer: I don't WANT to accuse schools of showing discrimination against the overweight children in their schools, but what else can we conclude? The kids doing a LOT of the bullying nowadays are usually the kids that our schools and teachers LOVE…the athletes and the popular kids. The days of the stereotypical bully…the big, mean, long haired kid from shop class…no friends, bad home life, no desire to vent his anger on the athletic field…are over. Those kids still exist but they have been overshadowed and outnumbered by the elite bullies of the 21st century. Attractive kids from good homes, the ones who form cliques of similar kids in order to protect the species…athletes who give the school good press by their feats of physical prowess…the cheerleaders (do I need to say more about THAT group?)…the cyber-geeks who control the information pipeline in the school…and maybe even the smart kids, who were once themselves the victims of bullying but now, as education has taken a front seat in the success of the individual, they have emerged as bullies themselves…taking the aggravation and humiliation of YEARS of past torture and torment out on a whole new generation of unfortunates. Teachers love these kids, so what do they do when they see bullying? Maybe look away, pretending not to see? Maybe the

SCHOOL has an anti-bullying policy in force, but as I said in the previous discussion about the legal aspects of this phenomenon, without a credible witness like a teacher most cases come down to an argument of "he said, she said."

Adding to the anxiety that our kids are already forced to endure, what incentive is there for an overweight kid being bullied to speak out? If the complaint is just going to be overlooked, resulting in what may be even WORSE treatment by the accused in future situations, what incentive is there for our kids to come forward? Overweight kids have no allies…we KNOW school bullying is an epidemic…we also know that (almost) every kid has a cellphone with a digital camera and many of them carry those flip-style cameras around with them 24 hours a day, recording every little insignificant thing that happens in their lives…so why are more of these cases not being brought forward for the record? I think for the same reason that so many date rape cases never see the inside of a courtroom…the "his word vs. hers" syndrome, the humiliation, the accuser becoming an outcast or pariah within their social environment, and if found innocent, the very real possibility that the accused will repeat the behavior on another unsuspecting victim.

So whose fault is it that our kids are suffering this misery? Who is really the culprit, the one(s) guilty of making our kids fat? If you read my ravings about the social conspiracy that's going on in this country then you will agree that, to a point, EVERYONE is responsible for contributing to the deterioration of the health and well-being of our children. If we see what is going on and we agree that it is wrong, and we do nothing about it…aren't we all guilty?

But I think we can all also agree that the primary burden of responsibility for the health and well-being of our kids belongs to their parents. From the time they are born until the time they leave home, parents are the ones primarily responsible for the care, feeding, and EDUCATION of their kids. Now, admittedly I am not a parent so my opinion is that of an outsider; I have no frame of reference from which to speak, and I can't even say with any authority that I know what parents are going through raising their kids. A LOT of parents who read this chapter will get angry with me and dismiss what I say here with comments like "…easier said than done fatso…" or "…fat bastard has no idea how hard it is to raise healthy kids today…" To those parents I say YOU'RE ABSOLUTELY RIGHT…I know what I know from observation only…but in response I ask you: does it take a genius or even *a fellow parent* to see when mistakes are being made? Isn't the proof that you're doing something wrong (or not doing something right?) reflected by your kids' weight and health? Also, who told you that raising healthy, well-adjusted kids was going to be easy? So you're right…I am finger-pointing and accusing you of being largely guilty of letting your kids get fat…AND I am not offering any solutions to the problem. All I know is what I have seen and experienced: that my mother, God bless her, was able to do it; that my brother and sister-in-law, both full-time working adults, were able to do it, and do it well; that my sister and brother-in-law, who has his own major health issues to deal with, also both working adults, were able to do it;

and that a lot of my friends were able to do it. So while I may not know from experience what I am talking about, the experts agree that there are some rules and guidance that every parent should follow to ensure their kids are raised healthy and happy:

1. Determine what KINDS of food and in what quantities your kids should be eating, and incorporate that into their diet. Good eating habits are developed early, and even the pickiest eaters can be trained to eat right. I have spoken to several sets of parents about this…trying to determine what the BIGGEST obstacles are to getting kids to eat right, and one of the most common complaints that parents have is about what their young children will eat and won't eat. I can relate to this…my younger brother was a picky eater, and I can remember my parents sitting with him for HOURS at the dinner table, long after everyone else was excused, waiting for him to eat the food that was put in front of him. Despite their best efforts, my brother remained stalwart…there were just a LOT of things that he simply would not eat. Their solution was to keep trying…trying different foods to see what kind of nutritional things he WOULD eat…and when they found one, they would make sure that it was made available to him. After a while, they had a strange menu for him, but it DID include several foods from each of the four food groups…so even though he was eating food that was different from everyone else, he WAS eating, and he WAS getting a balanced diet.

2. Don't over feed your kids…! If my folks made a mistake with me, and I am not saying that my problems are their fault…it was allowing me to overeat. It was their responsibility to tell me when to stop eating, yet I was allowed to keep eating. It wasn't until it was too late…I had already learned several bad eating habits, the worst of which was portion control…that they began to take notice and tried to influence me to eat less.

3. The school's meals are nutritional and balanced BY LAW…so if you have any doubts about your ability to provide a nutritional diet for your kids when they are out of your control, let them eat school lunches.

4. Don't let the fast food industry raise your kids…just like we too often let the TV raise our kids and expose them to most social scenarios…because it's the EASY way to do it…we tend to take the easy way out of feeding our kids. If your kids' early exposure to nutrition is fast food, then don't complain when later in life (a few years later, when they are adolescents) they refuse to eat anything but fast food.

I remember well the "eating" rules my father and mother established for us when we were growing up. The ONLY times I remember eating fast food (before I was old enough to purchase food on my own) was when my mom and dad went out for a dinner or a meeting. On these rare occasions, my folks would allow us (or our baby sitter, when we were VERY young) to have pizza, or McDonalds. Otherwise, since my mom was a stay-at-home mom, she did all of the cooking and we were expected to be at the dinner table when the food was served. I can also remember how much grief and work it was for her, trying to schedule hot, nutritional meals for four kids of varying ages that are all going in different directions at the same time…who was at sports practice, who was at band practice, who was visiting friends, etc. Despite these difficulties, she did a GREAT job managing the food workload…what happened to me was completely my fault.

5. Don't let the snack food industry raise your kids. Baby food is mostly mashed fruits and vegetables…if that's the case, why then do we let our kids change from nutritional and healthy fruits and vegetables to salty and fatty chips, candy, and cookies as their primary source of snacking? Again, I suspect that the reason has something to do with laziness and convenience, and even more with our kids picking up bad habits from friends (the MOST influential group of people your kids will encounter as they grow). If you stock the house with good stuff to eat, and discourage eating junk food, then your kids will adopt good eating habits. If you have to…FORBID your kids from eating junk…! Don't say that's unrealistic…they're YOUR kids, raise them YOUR way…!

6. Establish an eating schedule and stick to it. This is one of the MOST important "Good eating habits" that you can instill in your kids. Experts agree that maintaining a normal eating schedule will discourage your kids from eating late at night, the absolute WORST time to eat. I know many of you are thinking about how busy your kids get what with sports practices and extracurricular activities taking so much of their time…let's face it, your family may NEVER all be in the same place at the same time for a sit down meal, but you have to try…! Set reasonable meal times based on their schedules and stick to it…and don't forget to factor YOUR schedule(s) in there too. If the family has to wait until 8 pm to eat together, then so be it…but no later than that. Insist that your kids make an effort to be home for meals…and make those meals comfortable, upbeat, and healthy.

7. Teach your children how to cook. This is no joke; the only way you're going to get your kids to learn how to eat healthy nutritional food for a LIFETIME is if you teach them how to prepare it themselves…and DON'T rely on the school's home economics program…do it yourself…! Think of the alternative: they never learn how to cook so they rely on takeout food their whole lives…MAYBE you will be lucky and they will go to the prepared food counter or salad bar at the local supermarket…but

sooner or later, their busy lives will force them to the fast food chains…drive through death…!

One of my favorite memories of my mother is how she encouraged me to learn how to cook by watching her in the kitchen. I remember how she loved to have company in the kitchen while she cooked, so I used to hang out with her sometimes. She started slowly by asking me if I wanted to add a spice to something on the stove or if I wanted to mix something in a bowl, but it progressed to her sharing her recipes with me and letting me mix one concoction or another from the raw ingredients laid out before me on the table. I learned EVERYTHING I know about cooking (and I am VERY good at it) from my mom…even how to follow a recipe and how to know when things are done cooking despite what the recipe says…!!

8. Don't teach your kids your bad habits. You may not like asparagus or leftovers, but don't let your kids know that. Remember, when your kids are young and developing their core values and behaviors, you are their primary authority figure. They will emulate you and your actions, so if they see you turning down food or choosing not to eat something because you don't like it…AND you announce it within earshot of them…don't be surprised if you end up raising a picky eater.

9. Beware the video game junkie. This one goes without saying; the X and Y generations were brought up on video games and for some kids the ONLY interaction they get with the external world is what they experience in that stupid, little, poisonous screen. Like TV was when I was young, video games should be a PRIVILEGE for your kids…something they EARN by doing well in school and doing what is expected of them around the house. When I was young my father had a strict rule about the TV…it did NOT get turned on until after dinner. We were not allowed in front of it until our homework was finished, we ate ALL of our dinner (I remember my younger brother missing a LOT of TV sitting at the dinner table with a plate of something in front of him..!) and there was a 4 hour morning and afternoon limit on watching TV on the weekends. That meant if you turned the TV on at noon, it went off at 4 pm until after dinner. Dad did this to get us OUT of the house and away from the "boob tube." Parents should treat video games the same way.

10. Foster a desire in your kids to participate in outdoor activities. Get them interested in sports or bike riding or kiting or ANYTHING that gets them outside and in the fresh air, even if it's walking. My mom used to make a game out of going to the store…when I was young (too young to drive) and she needed something from the store, she would challenge me to a race: she would set a time limit to see if I could get to the store and back

before time ran out. She made it seem like my help was the only thing she could rely on to get the family fed…false importance of course, but I didn't know at the time she was just getting me outside and some exercise. It worked…at least until I got my driver's license…!

11. Plan family activities or vacations that stress physical activity. I've never taken a family on vacation, but I do know that there are MANY opportunities…be they far away or close to home…to take family trips and vacations together that stress a healthy lifestyle. Take your kids to local historic sites and have them walk around reading the plaques…take them to zoos to see the animals…to flea markets or farmer's markets to "window" shop the tables. My dad used to take us to the Jersey shore for vacations and we always seemed to be riding bikes or walking with him to the local store for newspapers or milk and eggs.

The schools have to take some responsibility in the nutritional health of our children too. Our kids spend from 4 to as many as 7 (more if they are involved in sports or extracurricular activities) hours at school for 13 years of their lives…the most important years as well, for experts agree that the ages of 6 to 18 include some of the most formative years in a human's life. That being the case, our schools have a tremendous impact on the habits and characteristics that our kids pick up, adopt, and retain. Once again, I freely admit that I am NOT in the educational administration business…I am a part-time college professor who teaches mostly adults, my <u>primary</u> concern is ensuring that my students are 1) provided with and 2) assimilate the lessons that I teach. I really don't care much if they got a balanced meal before coming to class. That being said, it again does not take a genius to identify the problem or develop some solutions for it…!

Lunches: I respect and acknowledge their budgetary restrictions, but schools still need to do a better job of feeding our kids. Of course there are minimum federal and state guidelines schools must meet with respect to nutrition, calories, and fat content, but these are MINIMUMS…if we want our kids to grow up healthy and adopt healthy eating habits, we need to go beyond the minimums. Get rid of snack and soda machines that sell junk food and sugary soft drinks…! Install a full, self-serve salad bar in the lunchroom. Why not replace Friday pizza day (ooh, I'm gonna get some criticism for that one…probably from kids mostly…but for the record, I LOVED pizza day when I was in school…!) with salad day. How about vegetarian days…one day a week experimenting with all-vegetable menus and recipes which include no-meat proteins like beans, nuts, and tofu? How about teaching more nutrition in home economics class…and then maybe making home economics a MANDATORY class so that all kids get exposed to how to cook, how to balance a diet containing all 4 food groups, and how to prepare a balanced meal?

Health program: I won't use the example of the health classes I had when I was in school because that was more than 30 years ago and I am sure that nowadays things are WAY different. Back then we were AFRAID to talk about safe sex and only BAD girls and boys bought condoms…now I hear some schools have a box of free condoms at the front desk in the nurse's office. So let's talk about the basics…nutrition is NOT just a home economics subject, it is a MAJOR health issue in this country. In fact, it is an epidemic…if we as a culture started pushing subjects like abstinence and safe sex down the throats of our children when AIDS became an epidemic, why are we waiting so long to attack obesity and unhealthy eating habits? Think about it: both epidemics are deadly, but obesity affects 70% of the population…so which disease do you think your kids are more likely to get? Health classes need to be geared more to nutrition, exercise, and the adverse side effects of obesity…hard hitting lectures about things like high blood pressure, diabetes, lymph edema, and circulatory conditions. It may seem like a silly suggestion but schools can combine their standard sex classes with a discussion about obesity and loneliness…"killing 2 birds with one stone" so to speak. Personally I would have NO problem giving a lecture to a high school health class about what it means to be a morbidly obese man in today's society…and the lack of female companionship that has resulted. We used to have those "scared straight" movies about drunken driving and drug abuse (and maybe we still do…I lost touch)…so what's scarier to today's youth than the possibility of "not getting any"?

Respect, toleration and acceptance: The news is full of reports about kids being bullied…in the old days (I never thought I'd use those words…I guess Mel Brooks was right…in his own words, "…we mock what we are to become") bullies mostly came in the form of big, scary, sometimes muscled guys who would physically intimidate the smaller, weaker, smarter, or fatter kids for their lunch money, to feel superior, or just for laughs. Today we have bullying and hazing of all kinds in our schools:

- Clique bullying, where kids from one popular clique will bully a hopeful, someone on the outside looking in seeking clique entrance

- Social and emotional bullying, where kids won't pick on others physically but psychologically…with taunts, ridicule, and exile

- Cyber bullying, where kids will use technology to convey social bullying…maybe through a widespread and negative propaganda campaign using Twitter, Facebook, MySpace, and gadgets like cell phone texting and emails.

WAKE UP AMERICA…!! Our kids are committing suicide because of this kind of treatment…they are bringing guns and weapons to school to reap vengeance on those who treated them that way. HOW MANY SCHOOL SHOOTINGS AND DEAD CHILDREN WILL IT TAKE BEFORE WE FINALLY TAKE EFFECTIVE STEPS TO STEM THE TIDE?

The solution to this kind of behavior is teaching respect, toleration and acceptance. Of course lessons like these are <u>introduced</u> in the home but they need to be ENFORCED, EMBRACED, AND INTERNALIZED at school…! Lessons on toleration and acceptance should become mandatory and be incorporated into the curricula of classes such as social studies, health, and history.

Finally, STRICT punitive guidelines regarding bullying and bigotry need to be established…and parents need to be included in the development and buy-in of these guidelines. It must be made clear to everyone that this kind of behavior <u>will not be tolerated</u> in any form…and students and parents alike must be made aware of the academic consequences of this kind of behavior…censure, suspension, and ultimately expulsion.

Sport programs: If our kids aren't getting enough exercise at home, then we need to see to it that they get enough in school. Here are just a few ideas that me and my friends came up with brainstorming one day:

- I suggest more cardiovascular physical activity in gym classes…more outside classes like handball, paddle ball, tennis, and team Frisbee…and in the winter dodge ball, aerobics, self-defense and martial arts training (kids absolutely LOVE this concept, and the gym coach does NOT have to be a black belt to teach the basics), and even yoga and cardio-stretching.

- I suggest mandatory participation in sports programs such as intramural sports or team sports. This is a tough one when considering the logistics of it…planning facilities, supervision, the cost…but if your kid is going to skip gym class with a doctor's note his whole school life, and he/she refuses to participate in anything else except video games…what else can we do to force them to exercise?

- I suggest mandatory participation in some sort of extracurricular activities that require the kids to get some sort of physical exercise, such as marching band or student body events like bake sales, volunteering at local non-profit centers, decorating for dances or homecoming, and stage crew for the school play

- I suggest mandatory participation in local or regional community service programs such as blood drives, assisting the elderly or handicapped, recyclable collection drives, collection drives for the needy or less fortunate (there is always someone who needs help from a flood, a tidal wave, a hurricane, an earthquake, or a drought), collection drives for our troops overseas, local street clean up, municipal landscaping, and assisting local food banks.

I further recommend that whichever of the above suggestions you decide to implement that the successful completion of them be made part of the formal graded school curriculum and necessary for the student to graduate and/or advance in school. One of the best incentives to get a kid to participate is when successful participation is mandatory to pass…it can be made pass/fail based solely on attendance and participation, but at least it will get the kids out of the house.

I am also a proponent of mandatory physical testing for students in high school. We as a society have chosen to establish minimum passing standards for subjects such as English, math, and science, why not physical fitness? Are our brains more important to our continued health than out bodies? My conclusion is that no matter how smart you are, it will always be the HEALTHY guy who lives the longest. There should be minimum standards established that test coordination, endurance, and strength.

Finally, and this is a silly pet peeve of mine, but to our school administrators I ask PLEASE get rid of group showers…! How much more can it cost to install ¾ height partitions between the shower heads in the boy and girl shower rooms…including a heavy duty shower rod and curtain so our kids can have some privacy? By the time they are high school age we expect them to be mature enough to handle group showers and behave appropriately when using them…so are we putting them into this scenario to prove that point? Because if we are, then we are FAILING…!!! There have been enough instances of kids NOT behaving properly in group showers to warrant taking another long look at this strategy and returning to the days when each person could conduct their own personal hygiene in private.

To conclude this chapter, I'd like to send congratulations to groups like Sesame Street and their touring shows like Elmo's Healthy Heroes for making a concerted effort to provide our young children with lessons on health and nutrition and making it fun at the same time…! I have done some research on this program and others, and while I have not attended a show personally it seems to be exactly what the so-called "doctor ordered"…! The Elmo show is especially good for our young kids as it teaches lessons on exercise, nutrition, proper sleeping habits, and hygiene through the use of song and dance by your kids' favorite Sesame Street characters.

Chapter 10: Bigotry, prejudice, discrimination, and stereotypes in the entertainment industry: Are YOU guilty?

Recently the current First Lady of the United States, Michelle Obama, appeared on the Dr. Oz show and the host asked her the following question:

> *"From my perspective the number one greatest national security threat that we have is obesity. Do you ever think about it that way?"*

Now I am no fan of Michelle Obama, but I DO respect her efforts to reduce childhood obesity…she has done a lot of great work campaigning for better nutrition in schools, more physical activity as part of the curriculum in secondary schools, and more education aimed at children to teach them good eating and exercising habits. So here was the First Lady's one chance to REALLY shine in my eyes…because the answer to such a foolish question should be obvious. I was even questioning Dr. Oz's agenda for asking such a ridiculous question. Was it a joke?

True to her nature, the First Lady let her true colors show through…in a world filled with terrorists hell bent on destroying the United States and causing harm to its people, groups that hate others for no other reason than simply for the sake of hating, and more and more enemies developing weapons of mass destruction that could obliterate us in a blinding millisecond flash of light…the First Lady answered as follows:

"Well, absolutely…the number one thing that prevents

young people from the ages of 17 to 24 qualifying for the

military is obesity."

Well, there you have it: the First Lady of the United States of America has categorized obese people (and obesity as a condition) as "the country's number one threat to national security." **Since bigotry is defined as "…*having strong and unreasonable opinions of another person or persons*", I would have to conclude that the First Lady's opinion of obese people as the "country's number one threat to national security" is a "strong and unreasonable opinion" of obese people**…a RIDICULOUS opinion if you want to get specific about it! If you the reader were STILL questioning whether prejudice and bigotry against the obese exists in this country up to this point in the book, I hope you're convinced now…!

How far and wide does this prejudice and bigotry reach? Is Mrs. Obama an isolated example or is her bigotry representative of a significant part of the population? Back in chapter 5 when I talked about going out in public I introduced you to an informal (and unofficial) survey I took at a local convenience store regarding the public's opinion on obesity. Granted, the people I chose to survey were limited to JUST those going in and coming out of a New Jersey convenience store, so some of you may (and I'm sure my scholarly peers will) argue that my research is NOT representative of ALL of America; maybe people from New Jersey feel worse about obese people than the rest of the nation does…! Maybe people in California are more tolerant and accepting of us? Well, I decided unilaterally that my results ARE representative of the American culture…I surveyed young and old people alike…I surveyed men and women….and I surveyed thin people, normal sized people, and overweight people. I simply took the first 100 people who were interested in participating.

Another question that I posed to my sample population during my informal convenience store research project was this: when you see or think of a morbidly obese person, what opinion do you form about them? To ensure honesty and anonymity I developed a list of about 50 positive and negative human traits for them to choose from…they only had to circle the traits from the list while I looked away. The top-10 stereotypes about obese people, in no particular order, are as follows:

1. Lazy

2. Stupid, ignorant, unintelligent

3. No will power or self control; they eat EVERYTHING

4. Incapable, a failure

5. Sloppy and slovenly

6. Lacking in personal hygiene

7. Apathetic, don't care about themselves or others

8. Mean or abusive

9. Perverted; sexual deviants; something wrong with them psychologically

10. Uncoordinated, clumsy, lacking in athletic ability

Wow….that's some list isn't it? You should pause a moment here and search your soul…what are you thinking to yourself right now?

- All or most of those statements are true…being fat is a choice, not an affliction, and anyone who allows themselves to get fat really DON'T care about themselves

- Some of those statements are true? You've seen it? Some or all of the fat people you know have exhibited one or more of the behaviors or traits listed above?

- I have never made and I would never make any of those conclusions about fat people

If you find yourself guilty of either of the first 2 conclusions, then you are guilty of bigotry. Sorry if accusing you of being a bigot offends you, but the classic definition of bigotry is "…the practice of having very strong and <u>unreasonable</u> opinions about others." If you make universal conclusions about ANY group because of your personal experience with one or more person from that group…then you're a bigot.

Did you notice that not ONE positive trait made the top-10 list? The list I supplied to the participants in my survey included human traits like smart, wise, caring, compassionate, funny, attractive (no one chose that one), strong, and honest. The closest positive trait/behavior to make the list was "funny, great sense of humor", which came in at #14. That's the "all fat people are jolly" stereotype…one of my personal favorites…! I can assure you personally that while most obese people TRY to maintain a sense of humor about their affliction, we are DEFINITELY not all jolly…! So if a small sample of 100 New Jersey-ites feel this way about obese people, harboring such a low opinion about us…what chance do we have to be treated equally in the American culture?

I am being overdramatic you say? Making it sound worse than it really is? "It was only 100 people from New Jersey…how can you generalize an entire population with those results? Aren't you yourself guilty of stereotyping, by branding the entire culture as fat-bigots?" OK, that's a legitimate accusation, so let's expand our view and take a look at how overweight and obese people are portrayed under a popular nationwide microscope: the entertainment industry.

How about movies? Let's look at a few movies (I picked several, but there are HUNDREDS to chose from) to see how the fat character(s) was/were portrayed:

The Nutty Professors 1 and 2: No single person/movie dynasty ever did more to contribute to the negative stereotyping of obese people than Eddie Murphy and his Nutty Professor movies. In less than 4 hours of film combined these two movies portrayed almost EVERY ONE of the negative stereotypes in my list above…Grandma and her sexual perversions, the overeating and obsession over food, meanness and arguing, the disgusting bodily functions, and even the young "Hercules" character, the only child character in the movie, displaying several negative fat stereotypes by himself…! What a WONDERFUL role model for our children…be fat, act disgusting, and you'll be funny and popular…!

It should also be noted that I take particular offense to the Nutty Professor franchise because something happened to me that was just like a scene from the movie. In one scene the Professor Klump character is out on a date with a pretty co-worker (played by Jada Pinkett Smith) when a black comedian comes on stage (played by Dave Chappelle) and proceeds to ridicule the professor ruthlessly. Everyone got a big laugh out of it…and not only the comedian's audience…it was one of the biggest scenes in the movie. The professor got revenge later in the movie when his alter ego turned the tables on that same comic, but by then the damage was done. When I watched the movie for the first time I had flashbacks…to a night years ago when my friends and I attended comedy night at our local fire hall. We were seated on the edge of the dance floor, almost directly in front of the comedian…and when he saw me…well, let me just say that the scene in the movie was NOTHING compared to what I had to endure. I was completely humiliated…an entire fire house full of my friends and people who knew me and my family…HUNDREDS of people…all laughing at me. At the end of the night the comedian came up to me and tried to apologize…the old "no hard feelings right pal?"…approach, but I couldn't even look him in the eye…I was afraid if I did I would lock my hands around his throat and not let go until I killed him or somebody killed me. If I had a gun I would have shot him…and that was the closest I ever came to killing someone…and my friends, those who invited me out for the night, seated at my table…were laughing just as hard as everyone else, all at my expense.

Shallow Hal: Was this movie SUPPOSED to be a positive social commentary? Lots of people try to debate that with me, but look at the facts: the collapsing chair scene (from personal experience…not funny), ordering food at the diner scene, rude and insulting comments from Jack Black's character at the underwear counter in the lingerie shop, and those unflattering "non-hypnotized" shots of Gwyneth Paltrow in her fat suit, a Hollywood trick of which I am NOT a fan.

Austin Powers: Congratulations to Mike Myers and his "Fat Bastard" character, the single most offensive fat character ever portrayed in film…well, maybe second most offensive…I don't want to forget Divine's character in the movie "Pink Flamingos" or Darlene Cates' mother character in the movie "What's eating Gilbert Grape?"…both of which were SO offensive they were more like caricatures rather than characters so neither made my list. It was a toss-up deciding who was more successful in the negative stereotyping of fat people…Eddie Murphy with his Klump family or Mike Myers with his single Fat Bastard character.

Tommy Boy/Black Sheep: Chris Farley was one of my favorite comedic actors and my favorite Saturday Night Live cast member, but with all due respect to his memory he made a career out of humiliating himself…and by extension perpetuated the undesirable image of the obese. That's why I put his two biggest movies together. Neither was more or less offensive than the other…both were bad. My friends argue with me that Farley's being fat had nothing to do with the character…that the movies would have been funny no matter who starred in them. Are you kidding me?

I do have to scold myself…for the record. My all-time favorite SNL skit was Farley's portrayal with another entertainment giant, the great Patrick Swayze, who was also taken from us too early. Their dance-off competition for the Chippendale's dancing job in front of a panel of judges was one of the funniest scenes I have ever seen…!

Van Wilder: Only one scene from this movie to mention, but it underscores my point perfectly: the pool scene, where the morbidly obese guy, uncomfortably-and-insultingly squeezed into a Speedo bathing suit, does a belly-flop into the pool…bad enough as it is, but punctuated by the subsequent "whale noises" in the background while he was under water. Congratulations for that one movie-makers…!

Disorderlies: Yes, the racial minorities aren't left out of this list. A movie about 3 black hospital orderlies whose wacky hijinks put them into many funny situations…with all of the obese insults they could fit into an hour and a ½.

Big Momma's House: Thanks to Martin Lawrence for his portrayal of a physically objectionable and overweight black woman replete with disgusting toilet humor and the inevitable and seemingly inescapable fat suit. I think what made it worse for me was the fact that the make-up on Lawrence's character was HORRIBLE…if you're going to put someone in a fat suit or fatten their face with latex, at least make it realistic…!

ANYTHING made by Tyler Perry with his "Madea" character in it! I know what Mr. Perry was going for in these movies, and I LOVE the strength and family loyalty that the Madea character displays, but did he HAVE to make her obese? How about his spin off shows "Meet the Browns" and "House of Payne": why did he find it necessary to make almost every character in these shows fat and objectionable?

Lean on Me: A wonderful "coming of age" movie about four boys on a quest to see a dead body, but why (Stephen King, you are my FAVORITE author of all time, but I am talking to YOU now!) did the movie makers have to make the "fat kid" in the foursome so unlikable and unappealing? Maybe they thought that the story Will Wheaton's character tells during the movie about the fat kid and the blueberry pie-eating contest was supposed to redeem their failure, but it didn't work on me…in fact, that story only intensified my displeasure for the entire movie. Who cares that the fat kid got revenge on all of the normal-sized people? The image everyone will take away is the image of the fat kid vomiting on everyone…pardon me if I choose NOT to take pride in that depiction!

Fatso: Dom Deluise was one of my favorite actors, and his heartwarming story about a fat guy who falls in love and tries to rehabilitate himself but finds it impossible is one of my favorite movies…but sadly it doesn't do much to dispel some stereotypes about fat people…no self control…eating all of the time…despite what you might think, not all fat people suffer from those conditions. The scene when Mr. Deluise' character consumes $40 worth of Chinese food on his way home to drop it off was especially offensive.

Precious: Nice try to the makers of this movie for TRYING to make a social statement, but in my opinion they failed. Several movie critics found this movie objectionable from a racial perspective, but that aside…the film makers ALSO set back the image of fat people back about 200 years. Everyone in that movie is fat…and physically and morally objectionable. I especially like the scene where the main character Precious steals and consumes an entire bucket of fried chicken…shame on Mr. (director) Lee Daniels, for portraying us not only as ravenous gluttons but as thieves too…maybe I should add that to my stereotype trait list? Anyone who sees that move and does "the math" suggested by it will come to what conclusion?

Marty: I saved this one for last, because it is the only one in my list for which I actually have praise. This movie, the "Best Movie" Oscar-winner in 1955 actually DOES portray its main character in a positive light: an ethical, dedicated, and hard working guy; a kind and caring gentleman; and a good friend, relative, and son. The problem I had lies solely with the way he was treated by others in the movie, especially the dance hall scene and how he was ignored and avoided by women…and before I am flooded with criticism by women, men are JUST as guilty as women in their opinions of obese members of the opposite sex…!

So what do you think so far? Convinced yet that this country has a HUGE (pun intended) problem with obese bigotry? Not enough evidence yet? OK, let's look at television.

The TV industry is just as guilty as the movie industry, maybe more. With shows about fat people and portraying fat people as weird, abusive, resentful, stupid, and physically repellant, how can you conclude anything else? Once again, allow me to provide you with some examples:

- The biggest loser: Of all the shows about fat people, this one is FIRST in my crosshairs. If you don't agree, consider the title: The biggest <u>LOSER</u>? The producers will of course claim that this is a cleverly concealed reference to the show's "alleged" purpose, which they say is to get obese people to lose weight. Being an obese person myself, I would like to offer a slightly different interpretation of the title: that obese people are, by definition, losers…!

The show's participants are put through rigorous trials of physical exercise and extreme dieting measures. Most of the scenes show the participants in a largely NEGATIVE way: struggling, crying or complaining, grunting and groaning, and oft times FAILING (when a participant, enticed to cheat, is filmed engorging themselves on junk food)…much to the delight of the viewing audience I imagine, since the show is doing so well. I guess a lot of people in this country get amusement or a sick sense of joy from seeing fat people struggling. All I can say is how DARE the producers try to pass this show off as a positive social statement…!

- HUGE: Shame on the producers of this show too: HUGE was a show about a co-ed fat camp located near a camp for children of privilege and the interaction between the kids who attend both camps. Another thinly veiled attempt at social commentary but in reality a "who's who" of obesity stereotypes. In no particular order you have the angry, the weird, the stupid, the physically objectionable, and the "uncontrollable eater" models. Note: Anybody who tries to defend this show by referring to Haley Hasselhoff's "pretty-but-overweight" character as a redeeming quality or a defense of the show's positive message is just as delusional as the show's producers…! Thank God viewers didn't see any redeeming quality in this show either…it lasted only one season!

- Drop Dead Diva: This one is easy. A show about a previously thin but self-centered and unkind skinny supermodel-type woman dies and she is PUNISHED by being reincarnated in the body of a fat lawyer. What a GREAT message for our kids: if you live an overindulged and over privileged life you might die and comeback as a fat lawyer…think about what that says about our culture…need I say more?

- Dance your ass off: A cheap and insulting knock-off of the popular "Dancing with the Stars" dynasty…giving the American TV watching audience yet another chance to laugh at fat people shaking their "stuff" on camera…under the thinly veiled claim of "obese people showing off their dancing talents while getting some exercise too." Give me a break…!

- More to love: Another knock off, this one taking is queues from the popular "Bachelor" and "Bachelorette" series. I guess the producers felt that fat people needed their own chance to find true love...pairing an obese-yet-seemingly-successful man with 20 similarly overweight but attractive woman. They even got plus-sized supermodel Emme to host it…apparently in a sadly vain attempt to add credibility to the show. The bachelor and his prospective suitor-ettes were put through a series of everyday situations to see if romance would blossom. Must admit, I didn't watch this one personally so I can't comment on whether the participants were exploited for their affliction, but I will conclude with this: did you happen to check out the woman who won the show? She was the SMALLEST of all of the other contestants by at least 10 pounds and was herself a plus-sized supermodel…! Curious…!

- Here is one of my favorite pet peeves: <u>any</u> show about skinny people in fat suits claiming that after wearing a fat suit for a period of time they know what it's like being fat. I saved this one for last because it is the one example of obesity bigotry that I find most objectionable. A few include made-for-TV movie "Fat like me" starring Haley Cuoco or "former supermodel" Tyra Banks' show where she donned a fat suit for a few hours and cried afterwards…actually CRIED…claiming she now knew what it was like to be obese. Are you KIDDING me?

OK, trying to keep my emotions out of this and remain logical and reasonable, how can any intelligent person in their right mind find any redeeming quality in this kind of representation? To Ms. Cuoco and Ms. Banks and anyone else who has tried such a ridiculous experiment: How DARE YOU suggest that by putting on a fat suit and walking around for a few hours that you really know what it's like to be overweight all of the time!! Do you think that in a few hours or even a few days in a fat suit that you can get a real appreciation (I use that term sardonically) for the emotional, social, psychological, and even physical (in some cases) pain that we experience…or the constant humiliation and embarrassment…or the consistent bombardment by the media of the message "fat people are different in a bad way, you are less of a person than we are, and we like to laugh at you." **There is one glaring difference between the "skinny person in a fat suit" and the obese person who has to live a life in that condition, a difference that makes their claims to "knowing what it's like to be fat" invalid: they can take the suit off at any time and resume a normal life…we can't.**

This particular insult must be important to me because I have this recurring dream about it…a bevy of self-centered Hollywood supermodel-types…the Paris's, the Lindsey's, the Pink's, the Britney's, the Cristina's, the Katy Perry's, ALL of the Kardashian's…anyone who has ever humiliated anyone for pleasure…all of these women decide to appear in a music video (I don't know why a music video came into play, but as I said, it's a dream) and they decide that it would be funny to dress up in fat suits and go out onto the streets to see if they attract as much attention dressed as fat women as they do normally as themselves. They are out in public with this raunchy, raucous, stripper-type music playing in the background…they all do their best to entice the handsome guys walking by, promising the guys sexual favors and anything they want if they would just show the girls some attention…but nothing doing. All of a sudden the girls decide, in unison, to remove the fat suits so they can ridicule and taunt the guys who shunned them…a "see what you coulda had?" kind of pretty-girl revenge. Except when they try to take off the fat suits, they find that the suits are now part of their bodies and they REALLY ARE FAT…! Then in my warped version of this dream there are a few suicides and a lot of crying and tearing at fat rolls, before the devil arrives to take them all down to hell…! And that's when I wake up smiling and feeling great…!

…and those are just the OBVIOUS examples of prejudice and humiliation in the entertainment industry! What about the more subtle examples? Consider the shows where the obese character plays a SECONDARY role in the show? Ashamedly I must admit that during my rehabilitation from bariatric surgery and the follow-up diet/weight loss I was reduced to watching a great deal of television. At first the trend was unnoticeable but inexorably there: without exception, on EVERY TV show that included an overweight or obese character, the obese character was portrayed as obnoxious, perverted, dangerous, stupid, ignorant, uneducated, dirty, or (in many cases) the target of ridicule, humiliation, and scorn among the main characters.

I forgot one part of the entertainment industry that has had a LOT of fun and has made a huge profit at the expense of obese people: comedians. Fat people have become the favorite targets of comedians in recent years, and the fat jokes keep coming. Hell, there are even several obese comedians who have made a living out of humiliating and insulting themselves. Fat comics such as Ralphie Mae and Gabriel Iglesias, two of my personal favorites, regularly denigrate themselves to the delight of their audiences. This begs the obvious question: where do we draw the line between what is right and what is wrong?

Some people will say that it is wrong to make fun of anyone for anything…but then why have comedy? Why were we blessed with the ability to smile and laugh? No, I think it's OK…even necessary…to be able to poke fun and laugh at yourself. Haven't I been doing that in this book, as I shared with you all of the funny stories of my obese exploits? Just don't expect me to laugh any harder than the next guy just because I am supposed to be jolly…I am definitely NOT jolly…!

No, the line exists between the funny and what does damage, like the insulting stereotypes that plague our society. Spreading and perpetuating stereotypes for ANY group is wrong, and as a fat man I resent when it is done to me. Tell a funny story about a lazy fat man…OK…but to suggest that all fat people are lazy, well that's wrong. To conclude this chapter let me tell a story about a skit that Ralphie Mae used in his act, a particularly funny story he used to tell about a Chinese restaurant he allegedly patronized. Seems he went to this restaurant which was having an "all you can eat" special for its lunch and dinner crowds. As Ralphie told it, he went in and was eating, and eating, and eating, until finally the manager, who was Chinese, came out from the kitchen and told

Ralphie to leave…Ralphie would describe the scene doing his best (which was NOT good, making it even funnier) attempt at a Chinese accent…a small Chinese man yelling at him "You go NOW…you finished eating!" Ralphie's response to the man was "But the sign says lunch <u>and</u> dinner!" as if to suggest that he had stayed from the lunch hour and into the dinner hour…I remember laughing a lot at this image.

But why does it bother me? Because in one comedy routine it highlights both good and bad comedy…funny yes, but only at the expense of perpetuating several stereotypes…the most obvious being that fat people are obsessive overeaters and stupid (how many of us would really misinterpret a sign that read "lunch and dinner"?) and the other being that Chinese people are cheap. As much as I like to laugh, I don't find that kind of humor funny anymore.

Chapter 11: Respect, toleration, enlightenment and education

So what is the answer? Is there a solution? First of all, maybe we should start by asking what IS discrimination anyway? We know what bigotry is and how to spot it, but what marks discrimination? Simply put, if bigotry is defined as having strong and unreasonable opinions of another person, then discrimination must be defined as "acting" on those opinions. Discrimination is loosely defined as the unfair treatment of people because of a difference they exhibit or a quality they share…USUALLY in the form of race, ethnicity, age, sex, religion, or sexual identity. That having been established, is there anyone out there who has read this book to this point who doesn't feel that fat people are discriminated against in today's society? Let me highlight some obvious (and maybe ridiculous) but real examples:

If you ever avoided picking the fat kid for a team when you were in school, you are guilty of discrimination. This includes not picking the fat kid for teams, clubs, organizations, or even as friends.

If you have ever turned down the romantic approach of a man (or a woman) just because they were overweight, you are guilty of discrimination. Call it "personal choice" if that will make you feel better about yourself, but it is also one of the simplest and most obvious forms of discrimination.

If you ever avoided working with someone just because they were overweight and you felt (with no substantial proof) that they just were not up to the job, you are guilty of discrimination.

If you were ever declined life or medical insurance solely because of your weight, you were discriminated against.

If you were ever in the position to hire someone and you avoided hiring an overweight person for no reason related to the requirements of the job, you are guilty of discrimination. In fact, you BROKE THE LAW too.

If you were ever charged for 2 seats on an airplane because of your weight, you were discriminated against.

Do you need more examples of discrimination? How about these?

Airplanes: The airlines are constantly "downsizing" their airplane seats…even normal sized people can't fit into the latest generation of airline seating with any degree of comfort. This has been suggested as a form of "size" discrimination. Then, after making the seats too small for almost any normal sized person to fit into, some airlines have implemented a policy that if you are too big to fit into a seat you must purchase TWO tickets…this happened to me several times when I was still flying. What bothered me about this policy the most was that after I was forced to pay for two tickets the airline stuck someone in the seat next to me…the extra seat I was forced to pay for…! They got DOUBLE fare for that seat…!

The most publicized case of this discrimination was when film maker and actor Kevin Smith of "Dogma", "Jay and Silent Bob", "Clerks", and "Chasing Amy" fame was forced to do the same when he flew. It brought a great deal of attention on this form of discrimination…not to mention to the ridiculous furniture practices of the airlines…!

Cars: I don't mind if the car industry wants to make ALL of our cars economically and ecologically friendly…in fact, I am all for a cleaner and greener environment. But does "smaller" have to go hand in hand with greener? I'm glad I bought my truck back in the 1990's, because I don't think there is ANY mass-marketed vehicle that I can comfortably fit behind the steering wheel now…!

Furniture: Manufacturers….ENOUGH with the dainty furniture already…70% of us are overweight, start making some furniture that won't collapse when we sit on it. Furniture should be weight tested like ladders: the bare MINIMUM that a chair should support should be 300 lbs, and they should only go UP from there…!

Outdoor conveniences: This one is near and dear to my heart, as I worked in an industry for years that used these conveniences. Also popularly known as Porta-Potties or Porta-Johns, these are closet-sized lavatories that you see populating construction sites and outdoor venues like rock concerts and flea markets. I remember 20 years ago when the standard outdoor potty was big enough to hold a staff meeting in it…now they are barely big enough for me to squeeze into. Size discrimination again.

OK, so it has been easily established that fat discrimination exists, so what should we do about it? Is legislation the answer? Should we petition the government to establish equal opportunity guidelines much like those in the Civil Rights Act, the Equal Rights Amendment and the American with Disabilities Act?

Believe it or not, but the legislation already exists. According to a 2007 article entitled "Obesity discrimination and the American with Disabilities Act" written by Jennifer Staman of the Congressional Research Service (http://digitalcommons.ilr.cornell.edu/crs/26), obesity is a disability protected by the Americans with Disabilities Act (ADA) of 1990. That means, if someone is found discriminating against someone just because they are obese, they are breaking the law. It will be treated much the same as a case of racial, religious, or sexual discrimination.

The legal facts are as follows:

1. While there is no federal law that specifically prohibits obesity discrimination like the ERA (women), ADA (disabled), or Civil Rights Act (minorities), some obese individuals have successfully argued in court that they are protected by certain provisions set forth by the ADA.

2. Section 504 of The Rehabilitation Act of 1973 states that "…no otherwise qualified individual…shall, solely by reason of his or her disability…be subjected to discrimination under any program or activity…"

3. The ADA defines disability as a physical or mental impairment that substantially limits one or more of the major life activities of an individual, such as walking or working.

4. Obesity is, in and of itself, not considered an impairment under the ADA; however, the Equal Employment Opportunity Commission (EEOC) has further clarified the meaning of the term "impairment" as it pertains to obesity: severe obesity, defined as being 100% over normal body weight, is **clearly** an impairment.

5. Any obese individual having an underlying physiological disorder which is the result or a side effect of their obesity is considered as having a legitimate impairment under the rules of the ADA…these disorders could include hypertension (high blood pressure), circulatory problems, lymph edema, Type II diabetes, and muscular-skeletal conditions.

So what's the answer? Is further legislation the answer? With legislation comes the inevitable litigation…so is THAT the answer…overloading our courts with cases from obese people who feel they were discriminated against?

The answer is, of course, NO…first of all, I was never a fan of "forced equality." That's the term I have given to government quota programs that try to force…by law…organizations to develop "diverse" populations. This trend is most prevalent in governmental agencies where racial quotas are sometimes mandatory…but even in the private sector companies are being required to "force" equality into their operations…such as "minority-business enterprise (MBE)" and "women-business enterprise (WBE)" usage quotas in the construction industry. I do not advocate quota systems: in a "forced equality" society, shouldn't I expect that 70% of all employees in every industry be overweight? If that's the percentage of the American population that shares that quality, shouldn't every workforce exhibit a similar quality? I think most NBA games would be a LOT more boring to watch if 70% of the players were overweight and I think a "fat quota" among jockeys would all but destroy the horse racing industry (not to mention MOST of the horses…!). Unlike some people I am very willing to accept that my condition limits the kinds of jobs I can hold…I have no delusional dreams of ever becoming a Chippendale's or a ballet dancer, a male model, or go into professional sports…unless it's bowling…! (sorry, couldn't resist sneaking that one in…!)

Without going into a lengthy debate here about the efficacy of these kinds of programs, suffice to say that these programs are a breeding ground for resentment and ill will. In the words of a good friend of mine, "You cannot legislate inspiration…true inspiration occurs through education and enlightenment." No one likes to be told how to run their organization…being dictated to by an outside power that has no stake in the results is counterproductive. Operational business practices such as hiring, promotions, rewards and compensation, and performance recognition that are restricted by quotas have the potential to generate even MORE litigation…in the form of reverse discrimination lawsuits and complaints. That having been said, what is the REAL solution? I recall a quote…I cannot remember its source…politician, motivational speaker, or movie character...but it rings true here. Clearly we "…cannot dictate what people think…one cannot impose opinions" If someone is intolerant of a group of people, for whatever reason, no amount of legislation is going to change their mind. If they want to be bigots, if they are prejudiced, or if they want to discriminate against a group of people, the only possible solution is education and practice.

The best place to start is in the home. Parents need to teach their kids tolerance and respect for all people, and they need to reinforce that principle over and over again in their words and actions. When their kids go to school, they must correct them if they come home and exhibit discriminatory behavior…and maybe even establish rules about who they can spend their time with if a particular friend or acquaintance is the source of the anti-social behavior.

In school, curricula need to incorporate more tolerance training and education. Children should have equality training from as early as elementary school and classes should be included in the mandatory curricula through middle school and into high school. It should not stop there; even colleges should incorporate some mandatory tolerance training into its core programs. I do not think it is unreasonable to suggest that social interaction training be made a mandatory class in every year of a 4-year program.

In the workplace, the federal government has made it a mandatory part of every business' EEO training that diversity and tolerance education be incorporated into the program. Unfortunately many businesses treat this training as a distraction…or a restriction to productivity…in other words, EEO training is looked upon as a pain in the ass and a waste of time…!. Businesses need to internalize diversity training as seriously as most MBA programs do…and treat tolerance as more of a social norm than a threat of termination.

As a culture, we have a very long and unattractive history of being intolerant and prejudicial to those who are different from us. I am not going to suggest that this tiny little insignificant book is going to be the answer to all of your problems or is going to be the catalyst that drives social reform in this country…that would be a little egotistical of me wouldn't it? However, what I do hope is this: even though I have been talking about fat prejudice in this book, maybe what I have said here forced you to look at yourself in the mirror and realize that you are guilty of intolerance…maybe even bigotry. If I succeeded doing that for just one person, then I did what I set out to do…and I contributed to making world a better place …!

Chapter 12: Conclusion: A pep talk, some words of wisdom, a long term solution, and what to do with a lifetime supply of candy!!!

From what I have seen in society, it would appear that we, as individuals and as a culture, are on our own. So far we haven't seen much action from our government to step in and make change…unless you include First Lady Michelle Obama and her anti-obesity campaign to rid the country of (in her opinion) its number 1 threat to national security…! Certainly the entertainment industry is not going to change the way they do business, as long as WE keep buying their movie tickets and watching their TV shows and laughing at their comics or their commercials…and the food industry has us in their power: WE keep telling them what WE want, so they keep supplying it, and WE keep buying their food…they are making BILLIONS of dollars from US buying their junk food, why should WE expect them to change?

Do you see a trend here…a common theme? It's all about US…the ones with the POWER to effect change is US…the people…and just in case you think I am being overdramatic about all of this, allow me to offer you some more fun facts…for those of you who think I am making "…much ado about nothing":

1. On September 24, 2010, The Fox News Network reported on an international study that was conducted on 33 of the most affluent and advanced cultures in the world. Of the 33 "developed" countries included in the research, the United States was awarded the dubious honor of being

the "fattest." We have the per capita <u>fattest population in the world</u>. How's THAT for a reputation to be proud of? I know we always like to be #1, but once in a while maybe it's good to let somebody else take the top spot…!

2. In the same study it was revealed that in 70% of our population is either overweight or obese. It was suggested that if the "trend" continues, 3 out of 4 American citizens will be overweight or obese by 2015. (Note: the "trend" mentioned in the research was EVERYTHING I discussed in chapter 3 in this book…!)

3. According to the article by Jennifer Staman for the Federal Government, obesity is now, officially, an "epidemic" in the United States. In a study conducted in 2004, 127 million of us were considered "overweight", 60 million of us were considered "obese", and 9 million of us were considered "severely" obese…and these numbers have been steadily increasing for the past 6 years. Do the math and you will reach the same conclusion I did as I wrote this book: overweight people are no longer the minority…we OUTNUMBER normal sized people…we are like the Borg from Star Trek…"assimilation is inevitable and resistance is futile"…!!! (Sorry, but I couldn't resist that…! I have this repeating image of a bunch of fat Borgs….barely fitting into their skintight black Borg suits, with their stomachs hanging out over their Borg belts…if they even WEAR belts…

having to sit down and catch their breath after every assimilation…and I laugh my ass off every time I think of it..!!)

4. Our kids are getting fatter than we are, and faster. As school budgets drop due to cutbacks, schools find themselves unable to offer enough nutritional, low-fat, healthy choices to our kids. Parents, whose influence is understandably limited because of the economic necessity of maintaining a 2 income household, are allowing the fast-food industry to dictate what our kids eat at an alarming rate. Athletic programs in schools and communities are being eliminated or curtailed due to budget cuts or apathy. In some cases even gym classes are being phased out and replaced with more academia in order to keep up with other countries whose kids are outdistancing ours in subjects such as science, math, and engineering. Despite all of this, our kids are spending more time in front of the TV, more time in front of the video games, more time tweeting or texting…and less time outside exercising.

So let me offer some words of wisdom and some advice for those of you reading this book…and maybe even an appeal to those organizations with the power to help us dig ourselves out of this inevitable grave:

First, to my fellow obese friends: NEVER GIVE UP THE FIGHT…! Don't ever stop fighting this condition...because you CAN beat it. I may be thinner now, but just like an alcoholic will ALWAYS be an alcoholic and a drug addict will always be a drug addict, I will always be a food addict and a morbidly obese person…I now consider myself a "recovering" obese person…so take this advice. Keep looking for YOUR FORMULA…the solution that works for you…if Richard Simmons' Deal-a-Meal doesn't work for you, then try Medifast…or try a combination of the two diets. If you've tried NutriSystem or Jenny Craig because you saw Marie Osmond and Valerie Bertinelli hawking them on TV and they weren't a solution for you…keep looking. Try combinations and composites of several diets until you find the right weight loss nutritional plan for YOU!

If diets don't work for you by themselves, then maybe your problem is part psychological AND physiological…so why not try therapy? I tried it and it works for me. Maybe you have an emotional problem that causes you to overeat…how many of us admit that we eat when we are sad, bored, angry, or stressed? That's an indication that while you may STILL be a chronic overeater, the solution may be just talking about it and uncovering what your underlying appetite trigger is. The stigma that used to be attached to therapy that…

"People who go to a psychiatrist/psychologist are just CRAZY…"

…no longer exists. As humans one of our means to survival is human interaction: what do you think therapy is except human interaction? We ALL need therapy, whether it's lying down on a doctor's couch and pouring our souls out to a stranger or just confiding in a friend. If you HAVE a good friend that you can rely on, then make him/her your "diet buddy." Remember, a diet buddy is someone you can call *at any time of the day or night for support*. Some of the major diets incorporated this practice into their programs with limited success and they offer diet buddy "surrogates", but I think it's much better if you choose your own buddy…preferably someone who is close to you. I don't have anyone like that in my life and I wish I did…because I think having a diet buddy is one of the best diet techniques going. When you are down, or you are being tempted to stray off of your diet, sometimes all you need is an encouraging word to "talk you down off the ledge" or a sympathetic ear to complain to…or someone who can tell you "Don't give in to temptation…YOU CAN DO IT..!" I guarantee that you'll feel a WHOLE lot better getting it off your chest…that "weight lifted from your shoulders" feeling…!

As I have revealed here, I've tried almost all of the solutions suggested here…including bariatric surgery…and never found my REAL incentive until I sat down and wrote this book…and discovered that I have been an IDIOT for the past 25 years…THAT was my epiphany…! I read and re-read what I wrote here and realized that my life over the past 25 years has been a continuous litany of excuses and finger-pointing…and when I saw it on paper I was ashamed of myself…! Start a journal of your own…be HONEST with yourself and admit where your mistakes are…if you're like me, you'll feel so much better afterwards…for me, it was cleansing, almost therapeutic. It was like self-induced group therapy…I was the patient and the doctor and the other food addicts all rolled up into one.

Until you find your solution…and find yourself able to beat the fat demon…don't despair and don't roll over…and don't let others get you down. Obesity discrimination and prejudice is a fact of life…it may not be right, I am not condoning it, and I will continue to fight it with every ounce of energy I have…but we will continue to be the butt of jokes for some time to come. You can't legislate what people think or make opinions illegal.

Second, **to all of you normal sized people out there: your goal for treating those larger than you should be *toleration, acceptance, and respect*.** You may not consider yourself a bigot, but if you discriminate or are prejudiced against ANYONE because they are different than you (and that includes obese people), then you're a BIGOT…! Why do people feel it's OK to discriminate against the obese but not against other disabled people? Is it because you feel that we have brought this condition on ourselves? Our obesity is our own fault…something we have complete control over…and we CHOSE to be this way? Do you REALLY think we WANT to be fat? Do you think ANYONE wants to be disabled? If you do, then you're not only a bigot but you're an idiot as well. We all have dangerous personal behaviors we indulge in, whether it's overeating, alcohol, tobacco, drugs, unprotected sex, or those behaviors that are considered OK because they are accepted by society like extreme sports. We all have faults and imperfections…just try to remember that next time you feel the need to laugh at someone less fortunate than yourself.

Third, to our elected leaders, please wake up…! You have established legislation that regulates the sale and/or use of alcohol, tobacco, drugs, and firearms because of their potentially destructive powers…then why not legislate the food we eat? Ask yourself this question: are there more alcoholics, drug addicts, smokers, or overeaters in this country? As of September 2010, it was reported that 70% of the American population is either overweight or obese…can the same be said for drug addicts, alcoholics, or smokers? If you check the statistics I think you'll find that overweight people outnumber the members of ALL those other groups combined, and obesity is just as harmful a habit as those others, with just as many if not more adverse physical and medical issues that are caused by it. Food addictions and eating disorders are just as harmful and debilitating as alcoholism, drug addiction, or addiction to tobacco. People are dying from this disease or its related side effects by the hundreds of thousands, and the survivors are clogging our medical system with their ailments. What more proof do you need to influence you to step in and do something about it? Don't worry about those who will say they don't want the government legislating what they eat and when…that didn't stop you when you enacted car seatbelt legislation, did it? If nothing else, why not tax the HELL out of junk food, making it less attractive and costly to purchase? New York City is now doing that with oversize sugary drinks, enacting a MASSIVE tax on any sugary drink over 16 ounces in size…and Philadelphia is not far behind, voting down a similar tax by a slim minority in 2011. But don't stop there! You've taxed OTHER non-essential luxuries before, remember? Cigarettes in New Jersey and New York City now cost around $6.00 to $8.00 a pack… cigarette and tobacco taxes so large that the percentage of Americans using tobacco products has decreased dramatically…and how about those massive luxury taxes for big cars and mega-SUVs…? Consider it a good deed that will generate a HUGE source of revenue for more noble ventures like funding HEALTHY school lunch programs, HEALTHY NUTRITIONAL meals-on-wheels programs for senior citizens and shut-ins, research and development of alternative energy sources, and cleaning up the environment. Here are a few suggestions you might want to think about…some reasonable, some practical, some maybe not so, but all worth considering…and hey, I don't even want any of the credit for the ideas:

- A federal "watch list" of unhealthy ingredients…such as oils, fats, sodium, preservatives, growth hormones, and pesticides.

- The appropriate language and definitions that manufacturers can use in their advertising and on their packaging. Set strict standards for terms like natural, healthy, organic, and anything with the words "low" and "free" in them.

- Strict standards for the amount of unhealthy ingredients allowed in processed foods such as sugar or caloric sweeteners, fats and oils, sodium, and preservatives. These standards should be regulated much like the gas-mileage standards on luxury cars…any product that fails to meet the standards (in this case, the amount of unhealthy ingredients exceeds the maximum standards) will be taxed

- Warning stickers should be required on any product that contains large amounts of ingredients that are on the federal watch list. You warn us about how cigarettes can cause cancer and other respiratory diseases, you warn us about foul language and suggestive lyrics on album/CD covers, why not warn us about food that can kill us?

- Establish federal subsidy programs for companies that produce food that is reasonably priced and that also adheres to federal diet standards…the only way we are going to get these companies to start making diet, or low-fat, or calorie-restricted food that the American public can afford is to give them an incentive.

- A federal mandate requiring an all-you-can-eat salad bar in every eating establishment. Fresh greens are the ONLY food group that most diets admit can actually be eaten in excess, so let's get more vegetables and fruits in front of the folks who frequent restaurants…let's give them a healthy alternative to that big steak or that huge plate of pasta!

- TAXES, TAXES, TAXES: Unhealthy foods are simply too accessible and cost-friendly…so the ONLY way we are going to be discouraged from buying them is to enact a "fat tax" on any food that exceeds the aforementioned maximum allowable standards for dangerous substances. Believe me, the ONLY way you are going to get some people from buying cupcakes by the case is if they cost $5.00 a package!

Fourth, to the companies that provide us with the food we eat…especially the fast food chains and junk food companies…you better wise up before it's too late! You better start looking for other countries to sell your poison like big tobacco did when they launched their overseas smoking campaign to sell American cigarettes. If you don't wise up soon then (hopefully) the government will, and then it will be too late.

Why not just start by giving us a break? Why not put some of that money that you throw at the TV networks to air your commercials over, and over, and over again and put it towards the development of a healthier menu? I like to use the example of breakfast food: if science was smart enough to develop an egg substitute that is low in fat and cholesterol AND a cheese product that is fat-free and tasty AND a ham product made out of low-fat turkey that is also low in sodium AND bread products that are gluten free and low in fat…then WHY THE HELL IS MCDONALDS STILL PUSHING THEIR ORIGINAL EGG MCMUFFIN ON US? That thing contains ingredients that are ALL harmful to you…cholesterol, sodium, and fat…it's a heart attack waiting to happen.

(…and since I want this book to be HONEST to a fault, I have to admit…I LOVE Egg McMuffins…still do…I used to eat them 4, 5, or 6 at a time) If the technology exists to offer healthy food to us, why not do it? I promise you: if you make it, we will come (thanks to "Field of Dreams" for letting me steal a sideways reference). In fact, I would think that the first fast-food restaurant that decides to offer a COMPLETE healthy menu, replacing all of their unhealthy choices with healthier-but-still-good-tasting alternatives, will see a dramatic increase in sales. We WANT to eat healthier; we just need YOU to make the choices available to us…!

(This next suggestion may seem silly and largely futile coming from one little disgruntled fat man in New Jersey, but as I warned in my introduction I'm going to say what I think needs to be said, so here goes…)

Finally, to the American population as a whole: SLOW DOWN…! Why is it that people from other "developed" countries can work less hours, take more time off for recreation (and vacations), and spend more time with their children while STILL maintaining a healthy economy and positive standard of living? Why can't we do the same thing?

One of these days we will wake up and realize what we missed…what we let slip through our fingers. In the great scheme of things…in the context of the long history of our universe, we all get about one microsecond on this earth…and what do we do with it? We spend it running around at a hundred miles an hour trying for "a better life." What is the definition of a "better life" anyway? Is it more money or possessions than the next guy? A nicer car or house? A higher ranking and more powerful job? Are those things the REAL important things in life?

Well, I don't want to wax philosophic here, but I can tell you from personal experience that the answer is NO…I was once one of you…pursuing the American dream of money, a big house, a pretty wife, and a big family. In fact, I was SO focused on the goal that I missed the race…and what it was doing to me! Before I knew it my ignorance (and my weight) caught up with me and I realized my mistake, but it was too late. I realized that I had spent the better part of my life "living to work" rather than "working to live." I was morbidly obese and even the simplest things…those that we all take for granted…were now out of reach. What I found to be TRULY important…female companionship, friends, the ability to function like a complete human being…I could no longer enjoy. Things I used to love…walking in the woods in the autumn, strolling the mall during the Holidays, holding hands, and sitting down at a table and really ENJOYING a sensible meal with loved ones…were now being denied to me because of my stupidity. I let the "race" take my life away.

Don't be like me…don't let yourself fall into the same trap. Stop and smell the roses before it's too late:

- Start making healthier choices for you and your family…eating, living, and working

- Get out and exercise…enjoy the beauty of nature while you can

- Put the emphasis where it belongs…on your health! It may be an overused and hackneyed cliché, but it's true…"as long as you have your health, you have everything"

I'd like to conclude this book with a funny story…something that has gotten many a laugh from my family and friends over the years. Several years ago, when I was working for that out-of-state company, I was driving the 2 hours down the highway to my office one lonely morning, just listening to the radio. Normally I was able to stay awake during my morning commute, but this particular morning I was struggling. Nothing I did was helping…not coffee, caffeinated soda, hard candy…including my never-fail, a crunchy bag of potato chips. I was still more than an hour from my destination when the DJ decided to have an early morning call in contest…the question was "What 80s band did the singer/songwriter Brian Setzer once front?" I knew the answer was "The Stray Cats"…and since I couldn't find anything else to keep me awake, I figured why not call the station and try to answer the question? Admittedly I should NOT have been using my cell phone in a moving car doing 70 mph down a dark highway at 3 a.m. …but I did anyway. I got through on the first try, some intern asked me what my answer was, and when I told him I was put on hold. A minute later the DJ came on the line, I was notified that I was on the air, and he asked me my answer…when I told him, he announced that I had WON…!! He asked me to stay on the line so they could get my info, and blah, blah,

blah a few minutes later I was back on with the intern, who informed me that I had won the GRAND PRIZE…a complete set of Women's Golf Clubs by Callaway…! Don't get me wrong…that's a NICE prize for a 3 o'clock in the morning radio promotion, but what the hell was I going to do with a set of women's golf clubs? I told the intern that I was not married and had no need for women's golf clubs and asked him if there was a consolation prize I could choose. He said there was but he didn't know what the runner-up prize was…and if I chose it I was taking my chances because prizes were not returnable or exchangeable. I thought about it for a second and figured "…anything is better than women's golf clubs…", so I told the intern that I wanted the consolation prize. I gave him my email address and phone number and I hung up.

A few days later I got an email from a wholesale candy company informing me about my prize. Apparently I had won *a year's supply of M&Ms candy* and it was ready for delivery. I remember chuckling to myself at the time, thinking "Well, I guess there IS something worse than women's golf clubs"…I was (and still am) a borderline diabetic and couldn't eat ANY of the M&Ms that I was getting. But I decided to take delivery anyway, because I had PLENTY of friends, family members, and business associates who I could share the candy with.

The delivery came 3 days later…2 cases of M&Ms candy…each case contained 12 large bags of M&Ms, each bag weighing in at about 3 lbs, 4 ounces for a per-case weight of about 40 pounds! That's 40 pounds of plain M&Ms and 40 pounds of peanut

M&Ms for a whopping total of 80 POUNDS OF M&Ms…! What a laugh we got from that as I handed out 3 pound bags of M&Ms to my friends at work…! **What I didn't know at the time was that the story didn't end there…*not by a long shot*!**

A couple of months later I got ANOTHER email from the candy company…the second *half* of my prize was ready for delivery. Apparently what I didn't know was that a "year's supply of M&Ms" as defined by the radio station was not the 80 lbs of candy I had already received but an "insulin crippling" 160 lbs of M&MS! I was amazed at the radio station's generosity…but who the HELL can eat 160 pounds of M&Ms in a year? Not wishing to look a gift horse in the mouth, I accepted the delivery again, figuring I could donate the candy to the folks who were unlucky enough to miss out on the 1st shipment (and there were a few) and give the rest away to friends of friends.

When my 2nd shipment of 80 pounds of M&Ms came, 40 lbs and 40 lbs again, something else caught my eye. Included in the delivery were several OTHER kinds of candy…5 pounds of chocolate covered raisins, a box of Snickers candy bars (48 candy bars in all), and a few other bulk candy products. I imagined it was a mistake, so I took it upon myself to contact the candy company to ask them how they wanted to arrange for return of the misdirected candy. They informed me that it was no mistake…the prize as it was purchased from them BY THE RADIO STATION was ACTUALLY a year's supply of assorted candy…so the extra items were mine to keep. "Oh well…" I thought to myself "…it won't go to waste…!" Once again I became the company's "candy man"….not to mention a very popular guy. I called myself "Billy Wonka" and started handing candy out by the boxful. Once again I mistakenly thought that my candy nightmare was over, and again I was wrong.

A few more months went by and again I get an email from the candy company announcing another impending delivery…and now I figured that something had gone very wrong. First of all, the contest I won was MORE than a year in the past…so my "year's supply" ended a few months earlier. Second, considering how much candy I had already received (in excess of 200 pounds, including the 160 pounds of M&Ms), I couldn't imagine any reasonable person thinking that a year's supply of candy should be more than that. So I called (again) the candy company to notify them of their mistake and was FINALLY given the real story:

The president of the candy company got on the phone with me and asked if I was cancelling my prize…I immediately said "No"…I was simply calling them to let them know that the year was over and my prize should have expired. *That's when he told me that my actual prize was, in fact, a LIFETIME supply of candy…and as long as I didn't cancel it or try to transfer it to someone else (transferring was against the rules) that I would receive candy deliveries every so often FOR THE REST OF MY LIFE…!* So, for the 10 years or so that followed that phone call, up until about the end of CY 2011, every couple of weeks or months I would receive a candy shipment. Sometimes these shipments weighed in excess of 100 lbs, especially those which included my

M&Ms, shipped at LEAST twice a year @ 80 pounds of M&Ms each shipment. I received all KINDS of candy…from the what-you-would-normally-expect kind of candy to the unusual including:

1. Candy bars, all kinds….Snickers, Nutrageous, Milky Way, 3 Musketeers, Oh Henry, and Zero bars, to name just a few

2. Leftover seasonal candy from Easter, Christmas, Halloween, Mother's Day, or Valentine's Day…these shipments sometimes topped 120 lbs if the candy company had leftovers they were trying to get rid of

3. Gummy candies of all shapes, sizes, and consistencies

4. Cookies and chips

5. All kinds of hard candies

6. Fudge and bulk chocolate for cooking, and

7. Chocolate covered EVERYTHING…in fact, I am still amazed by the variety of things that some companies will cover in chocolate…! Chocolate covered gummy bears, marshmallows, jelly beans, coffee beans, and nuts of all kinds! One of my chocolate-covered favorites were homemade S'mores; some candy company, can't remember their name, made S'mores by taking graham crackers, stuffing them with

marshmallow crème, and then double coating them with chocolate…a little bit of heaven @ $9.46 a pound!

So what's the moral of the story? That God has a sense of humor? Maybe…but I look at it this way…sometimes life gives you candy, sometimes it gives you onions…the important thing is what you make of it…! Good luck to all, and thanks for reading…!